SPIRITUAL FRIENDSHIP

To CHRIS

ON THE DAY OF YOUR

PROFESSION IN LIFE VOWS

7TH F

FROM   IS AT

ST. ANDREWS.

WISHING YOU LOVE, PEACE + JOY.

KENNETH TSSF. Sandra

margaret.

Dennis

Steven
Sue.

First published in 1993 by The Upper Room, Nashville, Tennessee,
USA. This edition published in 1994 by Eagle, an imprint of Inter
Publishing Service (IPS) Ltd, 59 Woodbridge Road, Guildford,
Surrey GU1 4RF.

British Library Cataloguing-in-Publication Data. A catalogue record
for this book is available from the British Library

Printed in India by Indeprint Print Production Services
at Thomson Press (India) Ltd

ISBN No. 0 86347 129 3

SPIRITUAL FRIENDSHIP

A Guide for Prayer Companions and Friends

Wendy Miller

Guildford, Surrey

PHOTOGRAPHIC CREDITS

Front Cover   *The Visitation*, Gael O'Leary r.s.m.

p28   *Journey to Emmaus*, Gael O'Leary r.s.m.

p40   Candle, Joyce Huggett

p49   Fishing boat returning to unload its catch, at the exit of the river Jordan from the Sea of Galilee, early morning. © Sonia Halliday Photographs

p61   *The Holy Family*, Rembrandt, 163?, © Munich, Alte Pinakothek

p68   The Judean desert, west of Jericho, Sonia Halliday Photographs

p69   The Sea of Galilee from the west shore, Sonia Halliday Photographs

p77   A view of the Dome of the Rock and the Temple area from the Mount of Olives, Sonia Halliday Photographs, photo by Jane Taylor

p85   *The storm on the Lake of Galilee*, Rembrandt, 1633, © Boston, Isabella Stewart Gardner Museum

p89   *Jesus heals the blind man*, Rembrandt c1655–60, © Rotterdam, Museum Boymans-van Beuningen

p92   *Harvesting Corn*, Henry Parker (1858–1930), © Fine Art Picture Library, courtesy Newman & Cooling Gallery

p104   Ploughed Field in Cyprus, Joyce Huggett

p109   Mount Tabor at sunset (The Mount of Transfiguration), Sonia Halliday Photographs, photo by Jane Taylor

p116   Jerusalem looking up the Kidron Valley, Sonia Halliday Photographs

p120   *The Last Supper*, Rembrandt, 1635, New York, The Metropolitan Museum of Art (Robert Leham Collection)

p124   *Preparation day*, Gael O'Leary r.s.m.

p132   *Journey to Emmaus*, Gael O'Leary r.s.m.

p137   Yes to Life, Tana Riviere, from the chapel, Old Alresford Place, Alresford, Hants

CONTENTS

Foreword		7
Introduction		12

PART ONE: Spiritual Friendship

1. Attentive Companions		15
2. Finding a Spiritual Friend		21

PART TWO: Meeting with a Spiritual Friend

3. Beginning a Spiritual Friendship		29
4. Journeying Together		32

PART THREE: Being Receptive and Responsive to God

5. Beginning to Pray		41
6. Pathways into God's Presence		44

PART FOUR: Reflecting on the Gospel of Matthew

7. Introduction			55
Wk	1	Tuning into God's Presence	58
Wk	2	God comes to us in Jesus	64
Wk	3	Listening to Jesus	71
Wk	4	Some Spiritual Disciplines	76
Wk	5	Being with Jesus on the Outward Journey	81
Wk	6	Still with Jesus on the Outward Journey	86
Wk	7	Our Outward Journey	91

Wk 8 Jesus' Easy Yoke   96
Wk 9 Learning to Trust   101
Wk 10 Thinking God-Thoughts   107
Wk 11 Letting Go   112
Wk 12 Journey to the Cross   117
Wk 13 Jesus: With Us until the End of
        the Age   121

PART FIVE: Ongoing Spiritual Friendship

8. The Next Step   131

Appendix   138
Notes   140
Bibliography   143

FOREWORD

I have never met the author of this book. Even so, when I read Wendy Miller's insights on spiritual friendships, I found myself cheering and longing to make her material available to a whole variety of readers. In highlighting the value of a spiritual friend, she is underlining the importance of one of God's most precious gifts.

A spiritual friendship is a friendship with a purpose. 'Spiritual friends' meet, primarily, to listen attentively to one another's faith journey. While one shares what has been happening in their relationship with God, the other seeks to discern where God has been particularly present in their friend's experience and what his Spirit seems to be doing and saying. Spiritual friends, therefore, are those who respect and reverence one another. They often find themselves drawn to each other by a shared sense of Christian vision, a passion for prayer and the spiritual wisdom they perceive in the other.

We read of many such friendships in the pages of the Bible. One sprung up between David and Jonathan. These two men not only respected each other, they were bonded to each other in love: 'Jonathan's soul became closely bound to David's and Jonathan came to love him as his own soul' (1 Samuel 18:1 JB). This bonding gave birth to a commitment: 'Jonathan made a pact with David, sealing it by giving David his own robe and sword, his bow and his belt' (1 Samuel 18:4).

A similar relationship was forged between Ruth and Naomi. So much so that Ruth's commitment to her mother-in-law can be recited by many Christians:

> 'Don't make me leave you, for I want to go wherever you go, and to live wherever you live; your people shall be my people, and your God shall be my God; I want to die where you die, and be buried there. May the Lord do terrible things to me if I allow anything but death to separate us.' (Ruth 1:16)

The mutuality of this spiritual friendship is traced very movingly in the beautiful book of Ruth. Here we see the two women supporting each other through bereavement, transition and long periods of waiting and uncertainty. They are still together when their fortunes change. So, when Ruth re-marries and gives birth to her first child, it is Naomi we see taking care of the baby (Ruth 4:16).

In the New Testament, too, we see a similar spiritual friendship supporting and sustaining two relatives; the cousins, Mary and Elizabeth. The picture on the front cover of this book reminds us of the love and encouragement these two women poured into each other at a time when their lives were enshrouded in mystery. The picture is a favourite of mine and I am grateful to the artist, Gael O'Leary, for giving us permission to reproduce it. The picture is also available in card form and, as Gael observes on the back of the card, 'Often we too can experience a visitation of the Lord in our encounters with one another. The Lord in each of us can draw out and affirm the faith of another. The deep faith of Mary can be ours, and the conviction that with the Lord all things are possible.'

Is that why, in the Apocrypha, we are reminded that, 'A faithful friend is a sure shelter, whoever finds one has a rare treasure' (Ecclesiasticus 6:14).

I find it fascinating that Jesus himself forged firm friendships. His relationship with John has been well documented – not least by John himself who wears the label, 'the disciple Jesus loved' (John 13:23; 19:26). This telling phrase seems to suggest that these two men enjoyed a special closeness. This implication is reinforced in John's own account of the Last Supper where we find him reclining against Jesus with his head on his Master's shoulder.

Interestingly, Jesus seems to have enjoyed an equally close relationship with a woman. He and Mary of Bethany clearly valued one another's company. In the light of the way Mary anointed Jesus in preparation for his burial, I often wonder what Jesus shared with her as she sat at his feet listening so attentively. Did he tell her that his death was imminent? Did he draw strength from her empathy and listening love? We can do no more than surmise, but a close scrutiny of John 12 implies that Mary's grasp of what was about to happen to her beloved was vivid and real. She seems to have heard what the twelve failed to hear – that Jesus' triumphal entry into Jerusalem would pave the way for the gruelling journey to Golgotha.

If Jesus and these great men and women of God blazed the trail for such spiritual friendships, is it any wonder that many Christians today find themselves drawing strength and nourishment from similar relationships? I say 'many' because not everyone feels the need all the time. Yet many of us long for a close companion at various stages

9

of our life – when we are going through times of transition or when we find ourselves consumed by a curious hunger for God.

At such times, we may find ourselves wondering how to find a spiritual friend. In this valuable little book, Wendy Miller gives guidelines for finding such a person. She helps us, too, to establish the friendship and to use to the full our time with the person of our choice. In addition, she feeds us with ideas on how best to use our own times of stillness, suggesting ways of drawing near to God, of meditating on his Word and of keeping a prayer journal. The bulk of the book consists of an invaluable method of praying with and meditating on Matthew's Gospel. The method may be used by individuals who have no intention of sharing the fruit of their meditation with others. It has been written, however, with spiritual friends in mind. So those who do want to express the fruit of their meditations with another or in the context of a prayer group will find that the author facilitates such sharing.

So far, I have only used this material for myself. I benefited from this so much that, at some stage, I hope to return to the meditations with a view to sharing my findings with my spiritual friend.

Unlike most spiritual friends, *my* friend and I do not meet regularly. Alas! For those of us who live and work overseas, this is a joy which may be denied us. That does not mean, however, that we cannot enjoy the rich rewards of such a relationship. As Wendy Miller reminds us, we can communicate with a spiritual friend by letter. Or, as my friend and I have been doing for the past twelve months, we can share our faith journey with each other by talking into a tape recorder. My heart leaps with joy and anticipation every time I see a packet from my spiritual friend lying in my post office box. I know it will contain a cassette and that she will have responded to the insights and feelings I have shared with her. I know, too, that she will have shared snippets of her own journey with me and that, when I have listened, I will feel loved and understood as well as challenged. I will also have reverenced and prayed with the things my friend has divulged.

So I have no hesitation in recommending this book to missionaries and others who have been uprooted and live and work overseas. In fact, supporters of specific missionaries might like to send this book as a love-gift to someone who works overseas. I also recommend it to those who live in their home-land or in countries where they are surrounded by supportive friends. I pray that the book's ministry will be widespread and that, through it, Christians all over the world may discover that spiritual friendship can come in a whole variety of ways: with a brother or a sister, a husband or a wife, between parents and children, cousins or friends, with male companions or female, single or married. I pray, too, that all those who seek such committed, nurturing relationships will have the joy of discovering what they seek. Through the mutuality of such sharing, may relationships with God steadily deepen as we rejoice in the ministry of spiritual friendship.

Joyce Huggett
Cyprus
June 1994

INTRODUCTION

Early in his ministry Jesus invited persons to be with him on his journey. Mark tells us that Jesus formed a rhythm in his relationship with his disciples – a rhythm of coming and being with, and of responding:

> [Jesus] went up the mountain and called to him those whom he wanted, and they came to him . . . to be with him, and to be sent out.
>
> Mark 3:13, 14 NRSV

We tend to focus on the responding – the sending forth 'into all the world' of Mark 16. But Jesus included all three movements in the life of his followers: turning aside from our activity to come to Jesus, learning to be with him, and then responding to him as Jesus guides us on our outward journey. This time 'with Jesus' puts us in the place where we learn to listen.

Jesus continues to call us into the quiet of his presence, but we do not need to walk alone. Discovering another disciple whom Jesus has also called, and listening to what Jesus is saying in the times of being with him or her is what spiritual friendship is all about. I invite the Spirit of Jesus to guide you on your journey.

Wendy Miller
Harrisonburg, Virginia

PART ONE

SPIRITUAL FRIENDSHIP

CHAPTER 1

ATTENTIVE COMPANIONS

Spiritual friends come in all shapes and sizes. We find them in a variety of places and times in our lives. Spiritual friends are people who pay attention, with another person, to the presence and the movement of God in that person's life. They pay attention, too, to the response the other person is making to God, to his creation, to others, and to him or herself. Several spiritual friends appeared and helped the apostle Paul as he began his Christian pilgrimage. Ananias had the courage to explain to Paul that it was the Lord Jesus who had appeared to him on his journey to Damascus and who would help Paul see and be filled with the Holy Spirit.[1] Barnabas paid attention to the Jerusalem disciples' resistance to and fear of God's working in Paul's life. He facilitated a place for Paul and the others to meet and to embrace the grace of God among them.[2]

Persons with the gift of evangelism can be spiritual friends. Philip was open and sensitive to the spiritual search of the Ethiopian court treasurer. His sensitivity, born out of his ability to listen attentively to the Spirit of God, enabled him to discern where the Ethiopian was in his experience and to listen to his questions.[3] Our questions can also be signals of where God is at work in our lives.

Irene Bergg, an elderly, white-haired woman who led a Bible class for teenage girls, was that kind of spiritual friend for me. Irene prayed for me, wrote to me, and when my family moved for the fourth and final time into a home of our own, became the friend who paid attention to where I was on my journey home to God. I began paying attention to God as the Holy Spirit moved gently in the world of my questions about who Jesus was, what his life and death meant, and what meaning Christ's return had for me. With the gentleness, patience, and skill of a midwife, Irene attended to the birthing of spiritual life in me and helped me to embrace Jesus Christ, the Spring and Giver of life and the Way home to God.

* * *

Ever since the first man and woman in Eden chose to chase after a web of illusions spun by the great enemy of God and all of God's creation, we find that we are not at home; we are distant from God, from ourself, and from one another. We no longer enjoy the harmony and community of Eden. It is this alienation, the colossal divorce we all suffer, that fuels our anxiety and our addiction for something to fill the painful space within us and between us. Much of what we do is only a continual effort to drown the pain, to cram the space full with whatever the latest fad might be – even religious fads. But the space belongs to God and God alone.

We tend to interpret the longing we feel as a need to try something new, something else. But the longings are God-given, Spirit breathed:

As a deer longs for flowing streams,
so my soul longs for you, O God.

My soul thirsts for God,
for the living God.
When shall I come and behold
the face of God?[4]

When we do begin to take notice of our daily rush and stress, when we begin here and there to wish that life would somehow be other – these are God-moments in our journey. God nudges past our compulsive race to keep up with others and creates a quiet space for the healing song of the Holy Spirit to resonate with the longing of our inner spirit.

Digestion of such fleeting awareness is crucial. The whole authentic history of spiritual discipline in the Church and in all deep religious traditions is to aid human digestion of the Holy, so that we do not 1) reject its nourishment 2) throw it up by not allowing room inside for it 3) mistake 'artificial flavours' for the real thing 4) use its strength for building an ego empire . . . rather than for sharing in myriad form for the good of others.[5]

In his letter to the believers in Philippi, Paul helps them to see that God who had begun the good work of grace in their lives would also be continuing this spiritual activity in them.[6] This transforming work of God happens as Christ is formed in us.[7]

A spiritual friend can help us pay attention to this transforming work of faith, hope and love. Sometimes a pastor or a Sunday school teacher is able to assist us in this way. Eugene Peterson, pastor, writer and spiritual friend observes that most people assume that pastors are:

teaching people to pray, helping parishioners discern the presence of grace in events and feelings, affirming the presence of God at the very heart of life, sharing a search for light through a dark passage in the pilgrimage, guiding the formation of a self-understanding that is biblically spiritual instead of merely psychological or sociological.[8]

However, one does not have to be a pastor to be attentive to God and what God is doing. My family doctor, after gently examining a painful injury to my eye, remarked kindly 'While you are lying still, waiting for healing, always remember that you are as close to God as your eyeball is to you. Everything you suffer, God feels with you. Remember with the psalmist that you are the apple of God's eye.' His awareness of God's presence in my suffering and in the dark space of waiting for healing helped me to open my attention to God on a far deeper level than the healing of my eye.

And someone called Marjorie similarly deepened my awareness of what God was doing in my life. Marjorie had invited us to do some remembering. There were about twelve of us seated in the circle of chairs, participating in a faith nurture workshop designed to help us understand and use the new curriculum for children and adolescents in our local congregation.

'Think back over your life,' she explained. 'Reflect on those people and experiences that have influenced your faith development as a child, an adolescent, and an adult.'

After some time in the silence, my attention wandered back to my early teens. I could remember kneeling beside a big, old, iron-railed bed in the room I slept in when I was fourteen, praying that God would bring our family back together and that we would have a place of our own to live. The house where we were staying belonged to friends of my mother's. It was our third temporary home in six months following the splintering of my parents' marriage and the scattering of our family.

I remembered looking up at the brass light fixture hanging in the centre of the high ceiling, wondering if my prayers floated up that far only to drop back down to the worn carpet on the floor. God seemed distant. And from my teenage perspective, nothing seemed to ever change.

I also remembered the brief but significant nudgings I felt here and there during those early teen years, usually when I was not praying. There were some words from a hymn expressing love for Jesus written on a scrap of paper, which in some strange way had turned up beside my locker at school. I felt a stab of guilt because I was not ready to love Jesus, but deeper within myself I knew that a willingness toward Jesus was being asked of me. Sometimes when I stood outside looking at the night sky punctuated with stars, I seemed to be given an inner knowing that encountering God was bound up with my life, with anyone's life. At the time I did not realise that God was trying to get my attention. All I knew was that I was not ready to encounter God. That would probably have other consequences, perhaps allowing Jesus to make demands. My response at the time was resistance.

Later that evening at the workshop, over a cup of tea, I reminisced with Marjorie about that fourteen-year-old memory. She listened carefully, and then in her insightful way, asked, 'Have you ever thought that maybe God was the One drawing you to pray in your pain? Or that your question about God being distant was the beginning of a conversation God was wanting to have with you?'

Marjorie was not only creating space for us to pay attention to our faith journey, she was also listening as a spiritual friend as I reflected on my experience of God and my response to God in that period of my life. I began to see that the grief and loneliness of that time was also an opening onto something new and life-giving, rather than just a miserable memory. I could also see that the loneliness I had felt because of the separation within my family was an echo of that deeper loneliness we all experience – the loneliness that comes from being apart from God, from our inner self, and from one another.

CHAPTER 2

FINDING A SPIRITUAL FRIEND

The conversations with Marjorie and my family doctor were some of those unplanned, occasional encounters with spiritual friends. At the time I did not recognise either of these persons as such, but as I was reflecting on those people who had in some way paid attention to God's presence in my life, I realised what insight they had given me. My doctor's understanding helped me to see my pain as a place to experience God's care. Then there was the gift of a window Marjorie had given me through her questions – a window inviting me to look in on the delicate movement of the Holy Spirit during my adolescence and to see what my response to that stirring had been.

Such conversations may happen more often than we realise. Bits of the holy are embedded in the everyday, but most of us fail to recognise our encounter with God for what it is. We may think such meetings only happen at church, rather than in the supermarket, in our garden, or while we are waiting for a bus or a train.[1]

Today there is a renewal of the long tradition in the church for intentional spiritual friendship. In the face of 'frenzied, confused, everybody-working, emotionally and materially distracted and often broken family settings that increasingly dominate our culture,'[2] we are feeling a need for the kind of friend:

who can be with us not only through crisis, but through the more mundane times of spiritual attentiveness in our lives. Proliferation of such friendships perhaps can help shape, deepen, and stabilize the shallow spiritual infrastructure of the Church, aiding its renewal and unique service to society . . . such friendships do not require spiritual masters, just attentive faithful companions.[3]

Sometimes we are aware of God's intervention in times of crisis, and we remember such times with thankfulness and joy. Campfire meetings and testimony times ring with such memories. But a spiritual friend helps us notice God's loving presence in the everydayness of life.

* * *

Arthur was happily married, had two lovely sons, and enjoyed his work. He and Sally felt at home in the community where they lived and in the congregation where they were members. On the surface Art knew he had everything going for him. Recently, however, he felt the need for something more. He and Sally knew they were involved in more community and church activities than they really wanted, but there did not seem to be time to think about where all of this constant motion was taking them or their children. Although it was gratifying to be well-liked and respected by his friends and peers, Art had to admit that he was tired of so much busyness. And when he thought about his prayer life, it felt like a desert.

His pastor began to notice that Art was not the only man in the congregation who found little time to pay attention to his spiritual life. He decided to offer an evening gathering for men who would be interested in deepening their discipleship. As part of the experience, the pastor invited the men to pair up and make a commitment to meet and share their life and spiritual awareness together. Art and Stan decided they could meet once a month over breakfast on Saturday morning. As Art began paying attention to his prayer life, he felt a growing freedom to think about letting go of those responsibilities that kept him busier than he knew was healthy for him or for his family.

Jenny had just completed a women's Bible study course and noticed how her spiritual attentiveness had developed as she experienced the prayer and scripture meditations. But now that the course was over, Jenny felt the need for some continued kind of structure or accountability. When she noticed a Sunday school class on spiritual friendship being offered, Jenny decided to attend. As part of the course, persons were invited to consider finding a spiritual friend with whom to share their pilgrimage. After praying for some help and guidance, Jenny decided to get in touch with a woman she knew in another congregation. They began by meeting every two weeks.

Gwen had just moved into a new town and felt the need for a spiritual friend. She knew very few people in the local community or in the congregation she decided to attend. During those early months of adjustment, Gwen began praying for God's help in her search. After some time she felt drawn to a woman in the congregation, a person she had met only briefly, but someone who seemed to care about prayer and the inner life of discipleship. Gwen decided to ask Adelle if she would meet over a cup of tea to talk about spiritual friendship. As it happened, the woman with whom Adelle had enjoyed meeting for some years had recently moved, and Adelle was also praying for someone else to meet with. A new friendship was begun.

*   *   *

It is my experience that I find what I look for. I begin to notice what I am paying attention to – whether it be yellow crocuses bursting through the snow in March, or God's invitations to come and listen scattered throughout the Bible. When I began my own search for a spiritual friend, I became aware of others who were interested in the same soul journey.

You may be wondering how to go about finding a spiritual friend. Or you may be searching for a small group committed to helping one another pay attention to God's presence in their lives and assisting each other to recognise their reactions and responses to God. While such friendships are beginning to emerge, the rediscovery of the ancient and biblical practice of spiritual or soul friendship is still new enough that you may not know where to look or how to start looking.

Begin by asking for God's help in your quest. Spend time in quiet before God. First tell him about your desire, and then wait in the stillness to hear what he has to share with you. You may find the name of someone coming to mind. You may wait in the silence and find that nothing comes to mind. In either case, your journey has begun and is being assisted by God. Trust the Holy Spirit to guide you in your search.

As you wait, be attentive to the thoughts and

suggestions moving into your awareness. In time you will probably find some persons' names coming to mind. You may well find that one of these will become your spiritual friend, or, if several names come, they could form a group.

As you think about both being and finding a spiritual friend, as well as praying, consider the following qualities:

1. An ability to listen, to be attentive.
2. An ability to provide hospitality: making space for another to enter and be at home as he or she lays a piece of his or her inner life out for another to see.
3. Trust and acceptance: 'Someone with whom you feel free to unlock your heart and trust, and who will be able to help you focus . . . on your spiritual journey.'[4]
4. A willingness to be accountable.
5. A willingness to pray and to allow one's life to be changed and transformed through the grace of God.
6. An openness to God and the movement of God's Spirit.
7. A sense of humour.

This search is a journey in itself. You may be blessed with the gift of a soul friend early in your quest. Often the search takes a little longer. My first experience of finding a spiritual friend took two years. Part of that length of time was due to the fact that I was not completely sure just what spiritual friendship was about or what questions could help me in my search. But my journey also took longer because I was resisting the risk of revealing my inner self to another.

PART TWO

MEETING WITH A
SPIRITUAL FRIEND

CHAPTER 3

BEGINNING A SPIRITUAL FRIENDSHIP

When you feel ready to approach someone about entering into a mutual journey of soul friendship – whether one to one or in a small group – you will find it helpful to meet and explore the possibilities.

If you are deciding to use a guide such as this book, or even if you decide to be more nonstructured, your commitment to each other will become clearer as you discuss the following questions:

How often are we able and willing to meet?
Some persons meet each week, others every two or three weeks, and some once a month. I know of some spiritual friends who are not able to meet even monthly but telephone and write to each other to stay in touch.

How long should our meetings be?
If both of you are going to be sharing your journey, you may need more than an hour.

Where will we meet?
Some people meet in a quiet area of a restaurant over a cup of tea or a meal.

Others like to meet where there is privacy and quiet – free from interruption from the phone or other intrusions. For some this can be in a living room, for others a quiet room in a church. Yet others prefer to go for a peaceful walk.

What kind of time commitment can we make to begin?

This handbook is designed for a three-month journey – enough time to know if you are beginning to feel comfortable with each other and to decide if you would like to continue or discontinue meeting. This kind of trial period will give you the freedom and space to know if any tension stems from your own fear of disclosure or from a sense that the relationship is not working.[1]

* * *

As we consider connecting with a spiritual friend, we may well discover some hesitation within. Our spiritual life emerges from the depths of who we are. If we bring its movements into the light of another's gaze, what might happen?

Like Adam and Eve in Eden, we fear being discovered. We are also fearful of change.

> I might be led to change my way of seeing and behaving. There is something in us that stubbornly resists this possibility . . . Why not let corporate worship, personal prayer, and my own discernment be sufficient?[2]

If we are honest with ourselves, we have to admit that we like to be in control.

> I procrastinated. It didn't take me long to get to the root of my reluctance. I didn't want to share what was most essential to me . . . What

I detected in myself was ... a battle with spiritual pride.[3]

Such fears tend to keep us in bondage to a self-induced isolation and move us further from the sense of community God invites us to enter. In choosing a friend to whom you will entrust your soul journey, you will find yourself confronting these fears with new courage – the courage to trust. 'Only those do we call friends to whom we can fearlessly entrust our heart and all its secrets; those too, who in turn, are bound to us by the same law of faith and security.'[4] This trust grows within the safe soil of a mutual covenant based on love, patient acceptance, confession, and obedience to Christ. As the hard shell of fear softens, the roots of trust and faith grow, and the gracious home for God, our true selves, and others blossoms in us and around us.

We are assisting in the continual birthing of spiritual life in the other, a birth that happens in its own time. We cannot push the pace of grace. Rather, a loving and patient sensitivity is called for on our part to be with the other as a friend, always aware that the same birthing is happening in ourselves as we surrender ourselves to the movement and transformation of the Spirit of God within us.

As we learn to be present to God, to open our attention to the God who is present to us, and to be aware of when we are not attentive and resistant to being present, then we will be more able to pick up on such movements in another. We are pilgrims together on the journey of the soul. We are learning to become aware of when we lose our place and of our need for a friend to direct us to the signposts God is offering.

CHAPTER 4

JOURNEYING TOGETHER

As you begin your journey as spiritual friends, you may need to spend time talking about how the journey will be similar to other forms of friendship and how it will be different. Such conversations encourage you to be open and honest about the kind of boundaries which need to be set. They also free you to move within the agreed boundaries and to discern what is appropriate or inappropriate. This is part of the process of building and maintaining trust. Agree to confront each other in love if you stray beyond the confines of the covenant you have set.

Preparing for time together

Keep your friend in your prayers. Pray also about your time together. And decide who will be the 'gatekeeper'. If one partner is more naturally gifted at keeping you both within the time you have agreed upon let them always act as time-keeper. If not, alternate. While timing does not have to be rigid or legalistic, you will both need time to share your experience. The gatekeeper keeps space open for this to happen, and for sensitive listening to take place.

Beginning the time together

As you meet, remember that you will both need a few minutes to settle into this time and space together. As we come into any meeting, we bring whatever has been happening in our life during the day, week, or month. Some suggested ways of shifting into the quiet in the presence of God and each other are included in Part Three under 'Spiritual Disciplines'. You may find it helpful to experiment with some of these suggestions and write ideas of your own as you move into the phase of listening attentively to each other.

Listening and responding

This is the time for making a space for the other person to walk into. We assist in creating that space by our willingness to lay aside our own agenda in order to listen with care and sensitivity to what our spiritual friend is sharing. Being truly present to our partner is harder at times than at others, especially if the events of our day or week have been especially stressful or energising.

As the other person reads, speaks, or is sometimes silent, we will be listening for the way God is working, the way grace is at work, how the image of God is being formed in her.

We will also be listening for her response to God: Is it a response of resistance or a response of prayer and action? It is only as we ourselves become more aware of when we are opening our attention to God and when we are not, that we will become more able to notice this activity in our friend.

33

> It will not be a matter of trying to remember what some book said to do and continuing a contrived 'helpful' response. More and more you simply will be with the person as they need you to be with them. Your own experience in touching and glancing away from the same Reality with which your friend struggles gives you a common bond and sympathetic perception.[1]

As we listen, our underlying attitude is compassion. As we are aware of our own resistance and response to God and others, we are slower to correct or to tell our friend what he is to do. We become open and quiet in our listening and respond by saying what we observe, rather than trying to jump to conclusions.[2]

One of our natural tendencies is to want to solve problems. It is an expression of our desire to 'help' the other person overcome or find some solution to their struggle. If we sense that our friend is not able to come to any resolution, we need to be aware of the helping responses that may arise within us. If we move into a 'rescuer' or 'parent' role, we will tend to take responsibility away from the other person and from God. A growing maturity will be evident as we allow the experience of the other to be open-ended and ongoing.

In spiritual friendship the shift is towards listening in the presence of God. If you are experiencing something of an impasse and no insight seems to come, you will find it helpful to turn to God and to wait in silence for a few minutes. This reflects an attitude of trust and dependency. We do not give birth to the answer for our friend. Rather, we are the midwife, waiting, assisting the process of giving birth to God's transforming presence in the other.

34

Sharing your experience

The basic content of what you share with your friend can grow out of your response to your reflection on the following questions. One question may stand out more than another for you. Do not feel that you need to slavishly work through the list each time you meet. The questions are designed only to help you become aware of movement in your spiritual journey:

What is my prayer experience like?
What happens when I pray or meditate on scripture?
What areas of my life is God touching?
How am I experiencing God's grace?
What is God like for me – in scripture, in times of prayer, or other times?
How have I co-operated with God this week (month)?
What am I not bringing openly before God's grace or love?
What do I need to confess?
What is changing within me as I listen to God?
What attitudes am I experiencing as I relate to others in my life?

In order to discover more clearly where you are in your prayer life, you may find it helpful to read to your friend sections from your journal (see page 50) you feel comfortable sharing. While journalling is easier for some to do than others, it is a helpful way to put out in front of you – in writing, doodling, or simple drawings and shapes – what you sense is going on in your spiritual life.

Finishing the time together

At the end of your time together, you may choose to pray for each other. You may want to mention those items your friend has asked to be held accountable for in the intervening time. Or you might like simply to sit together in prayerful silence reverencing and holding to God the things which have been shared.

Accountability

The conversation of spiritual friends covers all of life since how we relate to God finally affects every other part of who we are, how we relate to ourselves and others, and what we do.

As we sift through the various parts of our lives, we discover those areas where we feel God is asking us to change. One woman requests that her spiritual friend ask about her response to her thirteen-year-old daughter and to pray for her as she seeks to respond in love and wisdom. Another woman asks to be held accountable for her care of her own body, especially in the area of exercise. Still another person asks to be held accountable for his use of time as he seeks a healthy balance between work, relaxation, and prayerful solitude. Whatever the request, it is a sign of where the life of the Spirit is becoming incarnate, where the kingdom of God is being fleshed out in our lives. The intent is not one of harsh judgment but rather of making known where we are seeking to move in harmony with the Spirit of God within us.

We agree to be held accountable as we are ready. The focus of a small group, of which I was a member, was spiritual growth and mutual support. It took time for a deep sense of trust and openness to form, and some of us did not feel ready to be held accountable for a specific area of growth or action for over a year. The readiness of one or two seemed to help others consider where they could also be accountable, but the movement of God in one should never be used as coercion or manipulation of the other.

PART THREE

BEING RECEPTIVE AND RESPONSIVE TO GOD

CHAPTER 5

BEGINNING TO PRAY

Some eighteen of us were sitting in a circle exploring our earliest memories of prayer and how we had learned to pray:

'No one really taught me that prayer was talking to God, but as I watched and listened to others praying, I assumed that was what prayer was.'

'I learned to pray in church. We prayed prayers out of the prayer book.'

'My mother prayed with me at bedtime, usually a set prayer, like 'Now I lay me down to sleep'. But sometimes she prayed other prayers. I remember asking her to pray for my dog Trusty when I was about eight. Trusty had been injured.'

'I remember hearing my father pray in his study late at night, after most of us had gone to bed. I was so touched when I heard him mention me by name.'

As I listened I thought about my own journey.

I learned to pray by listening to others: a Sunday school teacher, a pastor, a youth group leader. For years I assumed that prayer was talking to God; bringing my requests, praises, concerns, confessions, and thanksgivings to him.

Like others in the circle, I saw myself taking the initiative to begin the conversation. But I had also seen the conversation as rather one-sided: persons who pray are doing the communicating while God is doing the listening. God's response would not be expected in the form of a dialogue or in the experience of his presence. If he responded to the prayer, then the request made would be granted. God could also decide not to grant the request, but in either case, he was seen as conversing with us through actions. This view of prayer tends to lead us into a one-way street. When we do all the talking, we are deciding how far we will walk along this street and what we will include in our baggage as we travel. We usually carry no more than what we feel safe revealing to God.

> Many people with an interest in religion have been traumatized by life and perhaps by false or inaccurate teachings about God. Their image of God is such that all they want is to keep on his right side or to keep as far away from God as possible.[1]

When our image of who God is has been marred by persons and events in our past, we will feel more comfortable keeping God at a distance, whether we are aware of our fear of him or not. If we add the guilt we feel because of our own sinfulness, we have another compelling reason for avoiding intimacy with him. It helps us to recall what Peter said, after a flash of realisation as to who Jesus was, 'Go away from me, Lord, for I am a sinful man!'

It also helps to recall that Jesus comforted him and calmed his fears.[2]

It is Jesus who calms our fears concerning God. When Philip expressed his longing to see the Father, he voiced the longing that has hovered in all our hearts down through the centuries: 'Lord show us the Father, and we will be satisfied.' Jesus consoled him by pointing to himself: 'Whoever has seen me has seen the Father' (John 14:8–9). Jesus came to make peace, to heal the rift, to help us know God for who he truly is – the God who is love.

It is this loving God who comes to us in all kinds of ways and begins a conversation with us. As we pause to reflect on the biblical story, we become aware that he initiates the relationships with Adam, with Abraham, with Samuel, with Moses, and with the children of Israel. In Jesus, he begins a conversation with us. John the apostle recognised God's initiative and wrote: 'In this is love, not that we loved God but that he loved us and sent his Son' (1 John 4:10). Matthew begins and ends his Gospel in the awareness of God's presence in Jesus Christ: 'Name him Emmanuel, which means, 'God is with us' and 'Remember, I am with you always, to the end of the age' (Matthew 1:23; 28:20). For the Gospel writers, this presence of God with us in Jesus Christ is at the core of the good news.

For reflection

- Trace some of the ways you learned to pray. Share these with your spiritual friend.
- Reflect on the way you view God at this moment in time. Share your findings with your spiritual friend.

CHAPTER 6

PATHWAYS INTO GOD'S PRESENCE

Certain disciplines can assist us in becoming receptive to God's presence and making a response to the One who is always present to us. Although the word *discipline* makes some of us uneasy, we use a large number of them each day – to eat, travel, work, speak, and play. We are so used to measuring the coffee that we forget that we once needed to learn how to use a measure. We can hardly remember learning how to count or read but we use and read numbers every day. These exercises are so much a part of us that we do not think of them as being difficult or dutiful. They simply take us where we need to go. Spiritual disciplines similarly form a pathway which leads into God's presence.

Many of us tend to think that spiritual disciplines are something out of our reach, something more suited for priests or saints.

'Far from it. God intends the Disciplines of the spiritual life to be for ordinary human beings: people who have jobs, who care for children, who wash dishes and mow lawns.'[1]

The spiritual exercises suggested in this chapter: 'Coming', 'Being With' and 'Responding' are to assist us as we enter into the Gospel of Matthew, walk with other disciples gathered around Jesus, and encounter him for ourselves. Just as Matthew pays attention in his Gospel to the many different occasions and places where God is present, use of the prayer disciplines will help us become aware of God's presence within ourselves and in the world around us. This awareness is both comforting and transforming. 'It is by being awake to this God in us that we can see him in the world around us.'[2]

This being awake to God in all of life can happen as we enter into the life rhythm of the early disciples. We tend to emphasise the going and serving. Jesus invites us to shift our gaze and to pay attention to:

Coming	'[Jesus] went up the mountain and called to him those whom he wanted, and they came to him . . .
Being with	to be with him . . .
Responding	and to be sent out . . .'[3]

Coming

We live complex lives. We think about one thing while doing another. We make plans for tomorrow while listening to another person talk. But just as those first disciples left their everyday tasks to be with Jesus, so Jesus calls us to walk away from the many voices and tasks that captivate our attention and energy in order to pay full attention to God.

These disciplines of 'Coming' help us to re-collect all the fragments of our body, mind, and spirit and to be still, open, and receptive in the presence of God.

45

Not all the suggestions will work for everyone all the time. We need to experiment to discover which help us open ourselves to God at any given moment in time.

Choosing a place

Throughout the Gospels, it is reported that Jesus developed a rhythm of retreat for prayer and solitude. He walked away from the towns, cities, and people to be alone in the hills, the mountains or on the lake. Often his disciples went with him. When they asked him to teach them how to pray, he mentioned, among other things, the need for retreat and solitude. 'Whenever you pray, go into your room and shut the door and pray' (Matthew 6:6).

Choosing a place to pray in our home assists us on many levels. It may only be a certain chair, but when we sit in that chair we know that our intention is to be open to God and to place ourselves in his presence. The other things we do in that place will also have one aim – to help us to be present to God.

Preparing to pray

After entering that place for prayer, one of the following suggestions might assist you to come more fully into God's presence:

1. As you come into the quiet place of your choosing, sit, kneel, or lie comfortably and still. Take some deep, slow breaths, breathing in and out very slowly. Feel your body relaxing. As you continue to breathe in and out slowly, allow your breathing out to be a movement of your letting go all that is

blocking God and your breathing in the receiving of all that is from God.[4]

2. Light a candle in your prayer place. Sit in the quiet, allowing the stillness and the light of the candle to draw your attention into the quiet. Allow the candle to be a symbol of the light of God's presence.

3. Play some music that draws your attention toward stillness. As you listen, feel your body and mind slowing down and entering into quietness.[5]

4. Stand with your feet slightly apart and your arms outstretched at either side of you. Move your arms slowly so that they are finally in front of you and your hands together. As you move your arms, reflect on the gathering of all of the pieces and events of your life and experience; and as your hands come together, offer them all to God.

5. After finding a comfortable place to sit, kneel, or lie, imagine yourself walking away from your daily surroundings and into the fields and hills where Jesus went to pray. Jesus is waiting for you there. As you come into his presence, notice what you bring with you. Whatever you bring may become the starting point of your dialogue with him. Jesus assures us that he meets us where we are, not where we wish we could be. Once the 'front burner' agenda is recognised and given its proper attention

> then we are more open and receptive to reading and meditating on the Scriptures.

Sometimes the dialogue that develops as we set down our baggage in Jesus' presence becomes the focus and content of our time in the quiet. Like the psalmist we are praying out of our experience, and we may wish to write our own psalm in our journal or to record what was significant to us in this meeting with Jesus.[6]

Being with

Praying the Scriptures

The Benedictines of the fifth century prayed with the Scriptures using a method known as *lectio divina* (which simply means sacred reading). Their desire was to integrate their prayer and their work. The steps to sacred reading are:

1. *Read the chosen passage slowly several times*, aloud if desired, allowing the words and phrases to linger within you as you read. The process is rather like eating a good meal. Enjoy the flavour of the words. Savour their goodness in the way you sample and taste different foods.

2. *Stay with the words or phrases* that catch your attention. Repeat them, turn them around in your mind, chew on them, if you will. Just as the food we eat begins to be digested and absorbed into our body, taking energy and nourishment to every cell in every place, so meditation allows the

scripture to be absorbed into all corners of our life and being.

3. *Allow your prayers* – of confession, thanksgiving, petition, worship – *to form out of your meditation.*

4. Finally, *rest in the presence of God.* Wait quietly and simply be present to God for ten to fifteen minutes. Various thoughts will intrude into the quiet space. Allow them to be, and rather than focusing your attention on them, return your attention to God. At the end of this time in the quiet, give a simple prayer of thanks.

Imaginative contemplation

Another helpful way of meditating on events and poetry in the Scriptures comes to us from the spiritual guidance of Ignatius of Loyola.[7]

Walk into the scene or story in the scripture and use all of your five senses to experience the event as if you were there. Rub your hands in the sand as you sit on the beach. Smell the fish the disciples catch. Feel the warmth of the sun on your back. Hear the conversations between Jesus and those gathered around him. Taste the bread and fish given by Jesus to the hungry crowd. You can find yourself becoming part of the story, not just as an onlooker but as an active participant.

Resist the temptation to pass over many passages superficially. Our rushing reflects our internal state and our internal is what needs to be transformed ... take a single event ... or a few verses, ... and allow it to take root in you. Seek to live the experience.[8]

When you *begin to move beyond your imagination*, you begin to encounter Jesus, and you discover that you are encountered by him.

Re: pond to Jesus in prayer – ccnfession, thanksgiving, petition, and praise.

Then simply allow the picture to fade and *be present to Jesus in the quiet* for ten or fifteen minutes. If your mind wanders, simply return your attention gently to Jesus. At the end of your time in the quiet give a simple prayer of thanks.

Responding

Journalling

Some of us like to write, others of us are less comfortable recording experiences in words on paper. However, some kind of written, sketched, or doodled reflection is helpful. It can help us begin to see on the page what is happening within.

> When we commit our observations to writing we are taking what is inside us and placing it outside us. We are holding a piece of our life in our hands where we can look at it, and meditate on it, and deepen our understanding of it.
>
> Beginning our work of observation by discerning our tendency to lie develops our capacity for openness and honesty, puts us in touch with our real self, and helps that self to make the movement toward becoming God's word in the world.[9]

Journalling can also be a way to converse with God by writing a prayer or a letter to him, or by writing a conversation with Jesus and 'listening' with our pencil as Jesus responds.

Some persons like a loose-leaf notebook, others prefer the spiral kind. Purchasing a notebook that suits your preference is one way of saying that you are paying attention to your spiritual journey. The content of your meeting with your spiritual friend can come from what you feel comfortable sharing from journal entries.

As you journal, do not be concerned about spelling or how the words or sketches or whatever you choose to express comes out on the paper. This journal is for you. It is a record of your inner journey and can help you discover patterns, needs, blocks and growth.

Recollection
Ask the Spirit of God to help you to see your day as he sees it. To help you focus, ask yourself:

How have I been aware of God today?
Where have I missed God today?
Where have I moved with God today?
Where have I blocked God's movement today?

PART FOUR

REFLECTING ON THE GOSPEL
OF MATTHEW

CHAPTER 7

INTRODUCTION

In this final section of the book, we enter into Matthew's Gospel and into his world.

Matthew reveals little direct information about himself, only that he was a tax collector before he was called by Jesus to follow him. However, this little piece of autobiography is revealing. On the one hand, Matthew's occupation lowered his standing in Jewish opinion polls. He was, after all, a representative of the Roman government that occupied Palestine. To the patriotic Jew, he was a traitor. To the scribes and Pharisees who had developed their own equivalent of a religious caste system, he was among the untouchables. On the other hand, his employment assured him a sizable income and kept him 'in' with those who were caught up with gaining influence and popularity and procuring the money needed to assure both.

When Matthew responds to Jesus' invitation, a deep and ongoing transformation begins. He no longer needs to find refuge in money and its illusive power to buy friendship. He becomes aware that God's Kingdom is larger than the Roman state that dominated much of the then-known world. As a Jew, he realises that what God had begun with Abraham and Sarah – the giving of a promise, the birthing of a people in relationship with God – God was now moving to fulfil. God is on the move, the Kingdom of God is here and coming. God is present to us in Jesus Christ until the end of the age.

Vast though this picture may seem, Matthew's eyes are also opened to see God in the everyday. The religious leaders had manipulated the Law of Moses so that any righteousness and acceptability before God seemed attainable only by scrupulous attention and obedience to the Law and the traditions of the Jewish elders. They had squeezed any life out of the meaning and intent of the Law, and in so doing had created deep factions in society between those acceptable in their sight – the 'righteous' – and those who were sinners and literally untouchable. As he continues to be with Jesus, to pay attention to what Jesus says and does, Matthew is deeply aware of a greater righteousness – the loving and merciful presence of God in Jesus, the coming of the Kingdom of God. This greater righteousness moves beyond the barbed-wire boundaries of the religious leaders and flows with mercy into the lives of people – healing the sick and mentally ill; freeing the demon-oppressed; embracing the untouchable lepers and tax collectors; empowering women; paying special attention to children, for their way of being and seeing is how we enter the Kingdom; bringing, justice and blessing to the poor; and congratulating those Gentiles for their faith in Jesus.

Matthew learns to pay attention to where God is moving in people's lives – through dreams, angelic visitors, boat trips, a boy's lunch, little children who want to be touched and held, conversations about washing hands, wine and broken bread, the cross; and above all, through Jesus himself.

The spiritual disciplines of meditative reading of the Scriptures using *lectio divina* or imaginative contemplation enable us to be present to where

God is moving, both in Matthew's Gospel and in the everyday world of our own life.

Arrangement of readings

The readings move slowly through the Gospel, allowing time for stopping to think and reflect. Although reading the Bible through in one year is a commendable discipline and gives a helpful overview of the Scriptures, such an approach can also be like trying to eat a five-course meal in a few minutes. Meditative reading takes small bites, enjoys the flavours and allows the spiritual food to be assimilated into all corners of our life.

To help us slow down and come to the Scriptures with an openness and attentiveness, a prayer of *Coming* is suggested. In the time of *Being With*, five readings are included for each week, with suggestions for reflection and simply being attentive to Jesus. On the sixth day some thoughts are given to help us reflect on the week and to highlight what we might like to share with our spiritual friend when we spend time together. The *Prayer Focus* is intended to accompany us each day of the week. Brief prayers like this keep our attention on God.

We have a tendency to judge ourselves if we do not complete everything every day, but there is no need to be legalistic as we read, reflect and journal. If we miss a day's reading, or even several days', we simply acknowledge that and move on. If we are only able to commit ourselves to some time in the quiet, two, three, or four days a week, we accept these limitations.

WEEK 1

TUNING INTO GOD'S PRESENCE

PRAYER FOCUS

Lord, help me to open my attention to your presence.

COMING

Before you turn to the scripture for the day, settle your body, mind, and spirit in the quiet, using one of the Coming exercises on p 46.

BEING WITH

Turn to the scripture for the day and listen to God's Word in a slow, thoughtful way. You may want to read the text aloud several times. Then, think through the questions and place yourself in the story. Simply be present; notice who is there and what they are doing. What is God doing and saying? How are persons responding to what God is doing and saying? How does it affect others? Who do you identify with? In what way is God present to you? How do you feel after this time of meditation? What shift has occurred in you, and where is it taking you?

GOD'S CARE DOWN THE YEARS
Genesis 12:1–5; Matthew 1:1–6, 16–17

Almost two thousand years are spanned by this genealogy. As Abraham and Sarah heard God's call to leave their country and their people to go to a land that God would show them, how little they knew of God's purpose! But they listened to God and began their journey. They discovered that it was a journey of trust and receiving, of believing God and opening themselves to receive the promise, blessing, and presence of God.

Over the years many other men and women became carriers of the promise and the blessing. Matthew lists some of them for us (Matthew 1:1–17); each one continues the journey begun by Abraham and Sarah, carrying the promise as they walked, stumbled, and sometimes fell. But God was at work down through the years, coming to them, being present, keeping the promise to bring the Saviour into the world. In Jesus all of us are blessed.

As you continue this time of *Being With* remember that you are also beginning a journey, a journey of trust and receiving, of opening yourself to God and what God brings to you. You will also be journeying with a spiritual friend, sharing your experience and listening to his or her experience.

Today, in your journal, begin your account of your own beginnings by recording those significant people and events in your past before you were born. You may have heard family members speak of these.

EMMANUEL: GOD WITH US
Matthew 1:18–25

Mary was pregnant but was not yet Joseph's wife – a scandal in the eyes of the town. Joseph was a good man; yet manipulated by fear, he decided to leave Mary (quietly) to carry the unborn alone. Then his sleep is shattered by the truth. The scandal was Emmanuel; God with us! Moved by God, Joseph opened himself to the risk of being a receiver of the promised blessing. He took Mary within his embrace and with her the Christ-child Jesus. What are the two names given to the baby, and their meanings? (vv 21, 23) How do the names speak of who God is for you?

Continue *Being With* as you are present to God in quiet attentiveness. After this time of waiting, you may want to bring other persons or concerns to God in prayers of intercession.

In your journalling, continue your reflection on your past by recording some of the stories surrounding your birth. Who named you? What do you know about your name(s)?

GIFTS FOR THE JOURNEY
Matthew 2:1–12

Reflect on these responses to Jesus' birth. Herod (v 3) and the wise men (vv 2, 10–11). How is God protecting the child Jesus here? (v 12)

Walk into the story – listen, touch, smell, worship. Some persons find they encounter God as they begin journalling their experience of the Scriptures and their inner responses to God. Conclude your time of prayer

with intercession for your family, friends, church, and world.

As you continue to reflect on your own beginning, add to your story the names of significant persons in your early childhood. Why were they important to you? What kinds of 'gifts' did they bring into your life?

DAY 4

BECOMING REFUGEES
Matthew 2:13–18

We are confronted with a tragedy and gross injustice here: the misuse of power in the hands of Herod, who represents the state. Here we see one of the faces of evil as it seeks to destroy God's plan in bringing Jesus to be 'God with us'. But behind the scenes and in the midst of danger, we find God protecting this family. Jesus and his parents become refugees in Egypt, even as God's grace is present to grieving parents in Bethlehem.

Enter the story; reflect on what you see and sense and hear. After a time of quiet attentiveness, conclude your time with prayers of intercession for family, friends, church, and world. Other instances of injustice might come to mind. Bring these situations and people and their needs into God's presence.

As you add to your life account, report on the important events in your life; the times of great change, of great sadness, of great joy. What meaning do these events have for you?

DAY 5

GOD HAS A PLACE
Matthew 2:19–23

For Mary and Joseph this is a time of looking for a place to live and in which to bring up Jesus. How do they depend on God for direction? God appears in Joseph's dreams (1:20; 2:12,22). Spend some time walking into the story and being present with Mary, Joseph, and the baby. Listen to Joseph's dreams and notice the various ways God makes himself known. Conclude with prayers for your family, friends, church, and world.

Complete your account of your beginnings by remembering the places you have lived (houses, towns, cities, countries). How have these places served to shape who you are today?

DAY 6

RESPONDING THROUGH REFLECTION

The sixth day of each week is a day to reflect on your journey of the first five days. You may want to come into God's presence as you do regularly.

Once you are still and centred, thank God for helping you become aware of his presence this week. Now read over your journal entries. Select a day on which you were most deeply aware of God's presence in your life. Bring this entry with you into the presence of God. In what ways does this insight/learning affect your life? What is your response to God? To others?

PREPARING TO SHARE

Collect the pieces of your autobiography to give to your spiritual friend during your time together. Reflect on which part of your journalling you would be comfortable sharing.

Reread Part 2: 'Meeting with a Spiritual Friend', as you prepare for your first session of sharing.

WEEK 2

GOD COMES TO US IN JESUS

PRAYER FOCUS

Lord, help me to open my attention to your presence.

COMING

Before you turn to the scripture for the day, bring all yourself into the presence of God.

BEING WITH

After you turn to the scripture of the day, listen to God's Word in a slow, thoughtful way. You may want to read the text aloud several times. After you have read the text, reflect on the questions, and then move into the story. Place yourself in the scene, noticing who is there, what they are doing, where they are. What is God doing? How are persons responding to God? To each other? Who do you find yourself identifying with? What is your response to God?

PREPARING FOR HIS COMING
Matthew 3:1–12

As you read through Matthew's Gospel during the next eleven weeks, you will be invited to sit and to walk with all kinds of people. They are people who are searching and waiting, people who do not always know what they need. As God comes to them in Jesus, their responses are mixed.

Where do you find yourself today? Who do you meet there? How does John the Baptist envision the work of Jesus? List the tasks that John expects Jesus to do (3:10–12).

What response to God's messenger, John, do you see and hear in people's lives? What response do you feel and hear within yourself?

This week, reflect on the times when you became aware of God encountering you. You may want to write an account in one sitting to share with your spiritual friend or to write a little each day as you follow the daily readings.

Reflect on this question for today: who are the persons who influenced my spiritual journey and triggered off any early responses to God?

BEING RECEPTIVE TO HIS COMING
Matthew 3:13–17

Now Jesus comes. Sit quietly and notice how he comes: receiving from John and receiving from God the Spirit and God the Father. Jesus is open to receiving God's gracious presence in whatever way it comes.

John is surprised. How Jesus comes to him is not what

he expected. Throughout Matthew we will see this gap between what people expected the Messiah to be like and what Jesus actually is like. The same is true in our own experience. Our journey is to discover what God is really like.

> Thou shalt know him when he comes,
> not by any din of drums,
> not by the vantage of his airs,
> nor by anything he wears;
> neither by his crown, nor his gown.
> For his presence known shall be
> by the holy harmony
> which his coming makes in thee.[1]

As you look back over your life's journey, record the God-moments in your life; those times when God seemed near and touched your life in some way.

DAY 3

JESUS IN THE DESERT.
Matthew 4:1–11

Now Jesus is led by the Spirit into the wilderness. Follow him as he leaves the crowds gathered around John in the Jordan River valley and hikes up the hilly slopes to spend time in the quiet of the wilderness.

He has been sent by God to save the world. How will he do it? What vision of ministry will Jesus develop in his time alone in retreat?

Satan presents several possibilities:

1. To use his power to provide for his own physical needs and, in so doing, lose sight of the deeper, spiritual needs that only God can satisfy (v 4). The focus here is not on

denying our need for food but on denying our spiritual hungers and longings in our grasping for food. Jesus addresses this again in 6:25ff.

2. To perform the spectacular and use God to bail him out of any risk in order to gain people's attention and thus prove God's presence (vv 6–7). Jesus refuses to manipulate persons or God.

3. To win the allegiance of the kingdoms of the world by worshipping Satan (vv 8–10). The lure of all that the world has to offer is dangled before Jesus.

Satan tests us in those places where we are most vulnerable. Jesus' place of testing had to do with his identity as God's Son (vv 3,6) and how he would do the work God had commissioned him to do. It is in the quiet of solitude that Jesus discerns the lies and deceptions being suggested to him. He leans on the Scriptures for guidance and for his responses to Satan.

Reflect on any 'desert times' you may have experienced – times of silence, aloneness, or testing – times when God seemed distant.

Where did you find strength and help during those times?

DAY 4

JESUS: THE LIGHT, SHINING IN OUR DARKNESS
Matthew 4:12–17

As you reflect on the places mentioned and on the prophecy of Isaiah that Matthew quotes (vv 14–16), what images come into your mind? Now place yourself beside the lake and watch Jesus coming (vv 12–13). What do you

see and hear as Jesus begins to preach (v 17)? Now what does the fulfilment of Isaiah's prophecy look and sound like? In what way is this a God-moment for the people in Galilee? For you?

As you continue to trace your spiritual journey, reflect on how you have come to enter into the kind of gracious rule of God's Kingdom. How has Jesus encountered you? What has been your response to him?

DAY 5

FOLLOWING JESUS
Matthew 4:18–22

You are still on the beach beside the lake. What group of people do you meet? What does Jesus ask of them? What

does it cost them to follow him?

What kind of God-moment is this for Peter, Andrew, James, and John? For the parents and families they left behind (v 22)? For you?

As you continue to reflect on your spiritual journey, think today about how you are becoming a disciple of Jesus. What have you left behind? Add these reflections to your account to share with your spiritual friend.

DAY 6

RESPONDING THROUGH REFLECTION

Reflect on your journey for this week. Become still and centred. When have you been aware of God this week? Now read over your journal entries, selecting an entry you would like to spend more time with. Bring this entry with you into the presence of God. How does it reveal God's gracious presence and work in you? What is your response to God?

PREPARING TO SHARE

Bring the written accounts of your spiritual journey together to share with your spiritual friend. Reflect on which part of your other journalling you would feel comfortable sharing.

WEEK 3

LISTENING TO JESUS

COMING

This week you are invited to join other follow-ers of Jesus as they sit on the mountainside and listen to him. Before you turn to the scripture each day, find a comfortable place to sit and settle your body, mind and spirit in the quiet of the mountain slope and the presence of Jesus.

BEING WITH

After you turn to the scripture for the day, listen to God's Word in a slow, thoughtful way, reading the text aloud if you like.

This week, since the readings (after Day 1) are teachings of Jesus rather than story, read the text until you come to a word or a phrase that attracts your attention. Stop and reread the phrase, savouring its goodness and nourishment in the way I describe in chapter 7.

We do not come to be with Jesus because we are righteous or strong. The people gathered around him because they were needy. In his sermon Jesus begins to explain the profound difference between the religious leaders' teaching about attaining right-eousness through their interpretation of the Law and traditions and the greater righteousness that moves beyond the Law to a relationship with God in Jesus Christ.

Our sinful, restricted self is uncomfortable and fights being revealed. But deeper within us is the longing for God that God himself planted there. We come to God as we are; caught by sin and longing for God; and we are always met by God's grace and mercy.

DAY 1

SITTING WITH JESUS AND OTHERS
Matthew 4:23–5:1

List the kinds of persons who gather around Jesus (4:24; 5:1). What is going on within you as you sit alongside them? Who are you in the crowd? Where are you sitting? Why did you choose to sit there? What is your experience of Jesus just now? Of God?

DAY 2

LISTENING TO OUR HEART-HUNGERS
Matthew 5:2–12

Much of our world's noise and activity seems designed to silence the hungers and longings of our heart. Maybe we are unaware of these deep, inner hungers. They are there, but perhaps no one has encouraged us to pay attention to them. Jesus speaks to these hungers of the human heart and to our inner longings.

If we listen to Jesus, we will discover that these longings are the doorways through which we come to God and through which God comes to us. Jesus says that the people with these longings are 'blessed'. They are welcomed into God's family. They are brought into God's kind and gracious presence and connected to one another.

You may want to make a list of heart longings found in verses 3–11. Which ones do you find within yourself?

Bring those longings into God's presence today.

DAY 3

FAITHFULNESS
Matthew 5:13–20

Salt enhances flavour. It preserves and cleanses. Light helps us see. It makes recognising God possible (v 16). Jesus is God's light.

Throughout the Gospel of Matthew, Jesus and his followers will be criticised by the Pharisees and teachers of the Law. These religious party members were convinced that by their practice of the outward forms of religious tradition and of the Law, they became righteous in the eyes of God. They avoided any awareness of their inward needs and longings or the inward longings of others.

Jesus calls his followers to a greater righteousness – or faithfulness as The Good News Bible translates it. He calls them to a righteousness of the heart. The laws of the Old Testament were given to guide God's people in their understanding of what God requires, but over the years the people moved towards maintaining the outward form and missed the true heart intent. Jesus says he has come to make the teaching of the Law 'come true' (v 17 GNB).

In the following readings from the Sermon on the Mount and in Jesus' teachings throughout Matthew, we will discover what he means by those words and begin to see what the greater righteousness – greater faithfulness – looks like. What God requires of us and what the society around us values are usually two very different things!

Where do your culture and your commitment to Christ clash at the moment?

DAY 4

ANGER AND HOW WE EXPRESS IT
Matthew 5:21–26

We have no problem agreeing that murder is wrong. But Jesus goes deeper, touching on the attitudes and motives of our needy self.

The call to a greater righteousness and faithfulness requires us to probe within. When do I become angry? How do I express my anger? By attacking and insulting others (v22)? Or in some other way?

As we open ourselves to God (v23), we become aware of the hostile attitudes we carry within ourselves towards others. Rather than covering up our hostility, Jesus calls us to make peace, to be reconciled. As we listen to God, we become more attentive to what is within.

DAY 5

REVENGE AND HATRED
Matthew 5:38–48

The greater faithfulness to which Jesus is calling us is not to keep a list of laws. We are coming into a family – God's family. The greater righteousness and faithfulness is to live in relationship with God and with one another

How does Jesus call us to pay someone back (vv 38–42)? How does Jesus call us to respond to our enemy (vv 43–44)?

As we learn such responses, we are showing a family resemblance (v 45)!

Bring to God any struggle you discover within yourself.

DAY 6

RESPONDING THROUGH REFLECTION

As you look back over the week, reflect on how God has been at work in your life. As you listen, what do you hear God saying to you? What is your response? In what ways may you have blocked God's voice? Where do you need to experience God's grace and forgiveness? Where are you still struggling?

PREPARING TO SHARE

As you come together, be attentive to each other, listen with openness and compassion. Share with each other how God has been at work in your life this week and how you have responded.

What commitments are you making and sharing with each other? For what do you choose to be held accountable until you meet next time?

WEEK 4

SOME SPIRITUAL DISCIPLINES

PRAYER FOCUS

Lord, help me to be present for you.

COMING

Before you turn to the scripture for the day, settle your body, mind, and spirit in the quiet. You may find one of the exercises on p 46 helpful to you.

BEING WITH

Turn to the scripture and listen to God's Word in a slow thoughtful way. The comments and questions for each day may help in your reflection.

Place yourself on the grass near Jesus and listen to him speak about spiritual disciplines. He invites you to an inward journey and describes some of the pathways into God's presence on the journey. Record your insights in your journal.

GIVING TO THE NEEDY
Matthew 6:1–4

Jesus begins with an outward discipline, helping the needy. However, he asks us to go on an inward journey, to reflect on our motives as we serve God in this way. The first stopping place on this inner journey is to discover who controls us. Is it God, or is it the people around us and what they think of what we do (6:1)? The task for us is to keep listening to God in the quiet.

We may pull back from the enormous need within the world, wondering what one person can do. Jesus simply asks us to give, to be attentive to the needs of others, and to be attentive to God who is present as we give.

Such listening to God opens our attention to the greater reality of the realm of his Spirit and presence. Gradually, we find ourselves becoming unhooked from the control of this world's values.

DAY 2

PRAYER
Matthew 6:5–15

Jesus withdrew from being with people in order to pray (Matthew 14:22–23; Mark 1:35). He invites us to follow him into the presence of God. When we do, we are once again moving into the world of the unseen, where Jesus lives and moves. He instructs us to retreat, to find a private place for prayer.

While we can pray anywhere at any time, Jesus still calls us to shut out the world's insistent beckonings by choosing special places and times for prayer. As you reflect on this passage, think about where you go to pray.

He then teaches a prayer that helps us understand a little of what the greater reality of God's Kingdom is about. You may find it helpful to pray this prayer slowly and reflectively and then to journal your insights.

DAY 3

FASTING
Matthew 6:16–18

While Jesus does not make fasting a commandment, he does include fasting in his teachings about spiritual disciplines. Our devotion to God is to be the central motive of our fasting.

> Fasting must forever centre on God. It must be God-initiated and God-ordained. Like the prophet-ess Anna, we need to be 'worshipping with fasting'

(Luke 2:37). Every other purpose must be subservient to God ... More than any other Discipline, fasting reveals the things that control us. This is a wonderful benefit to the true disciple who longs to be transformed into the image of Jesus Christ. We cover up what is inside us with food and other good things, but in fasting these things surface.[1]

Besides abstaining from food, there are other ways of fasting: abstinence from television, overspending, overworking, to mention a few.

How do you find yourself reacting to the challenge to fast?

DAY 4
CONTEMPLATION
Matthew 6:19–34

If we are not worrying about what other people think, then we are often worrying about something else: money (vv 19–24), or the things we need to live (vv 25–34), or even life itself (v 27).

Jesus gives us a simple but profound way to free ourselves from this kind of slavery and the worry that feeds it. He invites us to contemplate. As a first exercise, he instructs us to ponder carefully and prayerfully the birds and the flowers, both created and cared for by God.

Spend fifteen minutes in quiet awareness of the birds and flowers and trees. Simply be present to God and creation. Listen and be receptive to God's care and presence.

DAY 5
DISCERNMENT
Matthew 7:1–12

Jesus came to make the blind see (Matthew 11:5). He sees deep into our inner person and invites us to follow him as he lays his hands on those places where we hold on to attitudes and fears that distort how we see others and how we see God.

What is your heart's attitude towards people (vv 3–4)? What is your heart's image of God as you pray (v 11)?

DAY 6

RESPONDING THROUGH REFLECTION
Matthew 7:13–14

Jesus describes the way of life; it is narrow, difficult and lonely. We need the companionship of others on the road. Spiritual friendship lightens the journey, helping us to know we are among fellow pilgrims on the way.

As you reflect on the spiritual disciplines you have focused on this week, you may want to prayerfully choose one or two to continue using as you travel. Spend some time in those disciplines today.

PREPARING TO SHARE

After taking some time to come into the quiet together, share something from your inner journey with your friend. Listen for what God is saying and doing and how your friend is responding to God.

Share with each other the spiritual disciplines you are choosing to use. In future times together, be listening for each other's experience and learning in your use of those disciplines.

WEEK 5

BEING WITH JESUS ON THE OUTWARD JOURNEY

PRAYER FOCUS

Lord, help me to pay attention to your presence in the people around me.

COMING

As you come into a quiet place, still your mind and your body. Allow the rush and noise to die down. Choose your favourite exercise to assist you as you get in touch with your desire for God.

BEING WITH

This week, as you turn prayerfully to the Scriptures, you will be walking with Jesus and the disciples away from the mountainside and into the streets and homes where people live and work and wonder. In the outward journey, we begin living out what we have heard from God in the quiet.

HEARING AND OBEYING
Matthew 7:24–27

As you read these words of Jesus, reflect on the two kinds of foundations. Ask God to help you see what foundations you have learned to build your life on.

What does your inner security have to do with hearing and obeying Jesus?

Remember that on the outward journey your sense of security will sometimes be tested.

RESTORING THE OUTCAST
Matthew 8:1–4

Walk into the story today and be with Jesus as he moves towards the leper, welcomes his request, and reaches out to touch him. Notice also how Jesus makes sure this man is restored to community – an important part of his healing. (You may want to read Leviticus 14 to discover why Jesus told the man to go to his priest and offer a sacrifice.)

In what way do you need to be restored? As you come to Jesus at the bottom of the hill, what do you need to ask of him?

AFFIRMING FAITH
Matthew 8:5–13

As Jesus walks into Capernaum he meets another 'outcast' – a military officer in the Roman occupation army in Israel. Stand on the street in this town on the northern edge of Lake Galilee, and listen carefully to Jesus' reply to the man.

All through the Gospel of Matthew, we will be hearing Jesus respond to and teach about faith. Faith sees God's greater reality and comes into the community of the Kingdom of Heaven (v 11). As you walk with Jesus and your spiritual friend, your 'little' reality will begin to crumble, so that the greater reality of God's Kingdom can grow within you and around you.

What have you experienced of God's greater reality since you began walking with your spiritual friend?

DAY 4

FAITH AND PRIORITIES
Matthew 8:14–22; Mark 1:35–38

After you have read both passages, reflect on what it means to the disciples to follow Jesus. What concerns do the disciples have? Where does Jesus find his direction?

In the silence and solitude with God, Jesus is released from the many voices that clamour for his attention so that he can listen to the one voice of his heavenly Father. The spiritual disciplines of solitude and prayer free us to listen and obey (Matthew 7:24).

What are you hearing in the quiet?

DAY 5

STORM IN THE MIDST OF OBEDIENCE
Matthew 8:23–27

Today you are in the boat with Jesus and the other disciples, rowing toward Gadara, on the other side of Lake Galilee. In the midst of obedience, a fierce storm hits! The disciples' sense of security is threatened.

The 'sea' is a place of great peril and destruction . . . and although Jesus has mastery over it, it evokes feelings of cowardice, fear, and little faith in the disciples.[1]

Speak to Jesus about your experience in the storm and the boat. What storms are you encountering in your own life? Bring these events into the presence of God also. Then wait and listen in the quiet.

Make a note of your prayer experience in your journal.

DAY 6

RESPONDING THROUGH REFLECTION

As you look back over this week, reflect on occasions when you have experienced God's presence and what you have heard God saying to you. What spiritual disciplines are helping you pay attention to God? What is your response to God today?

PREPARING TO SHARE

Respond to the following questions as you prepare to share with your friend:

- What am I hearing God say?
- How am I responding within myself?
- How is my inner journey changing my outward journey?

WEEK 6

STILL WITH JESUS ON THE OUTWARD JOURNEY

PRAYER FOCUS

Lord, help me to see as you see, to hear as you hear

COMING

Take a few minutes to consciously place yourself in God's presence. Let go of the activity and pressures of the day and be still.

BEING WITH

This week you will continue walking with Jesus and waiting while he takes time to be present to people whom many others would rather avoid. You will also be present as people begin to criticise and reject him.

Listen to Jesus. Listen to the rejection. Listen to your own inner feelings and thoughts as you encounter persons who are difficult to be with and persons who reject and criticise.

RESPONDING TO OPPRESSION AND PARALYSIS OF SPIRIT
Matthew 8:28–9:8

After the stormy ride, you are confronted by two men whose lives are full of storm and confusion. They live in a cemetery and no one dares to go near them. But Jesus is unafraid.

Jesus accepts the presence of demons as a present reality rather than denying that they exist or refusing to respond to people who are oppressed by their presence. He listens to the demons screaming in fear at him and with calm authority orders the oppressive and controlling spirits to leave the men alone.

The people in the town ask Jesus to leave. Anyone casting out demons is a threat to them!

After returning to Capernaum, another man enters the story: a paralysed man who is carried by friends to Jesus. As you are present in the story, watch and listen.

Who is present? What inner longings is Jesus aware of in the paralysed man? What are the responses of those watching and listening? Which persons do you see living and moving into the greater reality of God's gracious rule, and which ones are stuck in their own self-righteousness?

What inner longings, debilitating oppressions, or needs for forgiveness do you want to bring to Jesus today? Journal your insights and learnings.

DAY 2

BEFRIENDING
Matthew 9:9–17

We continue walking with Jesus and the disciples through the streets of Capernaum. He invites Matthew to join him, a man who collected taxes from the Jews for the Roman occupation forces. He and many others were considered the untouchables in Jewish society. But Jesus lives in solidarity with Matthew and his friends as he sits and eats with them. Such solidarity brings criticism from the Pharisees.

In your meditation, listen to the responses within yourself. Who do you find it hard to be with? Difficult to listen to? Journal your insights and listen for Jesus speaking to you.

DAY 3

BEING SENSITIVE TO ALL KINDS OF SUFFERING
Matthew 9:18–26

While you are walking with Jesus on the streets of Capernaum, two more persons with great need come to him: a father whose daughter has just died and a woman who has been severely ill for twelve years. Jesus hears their prayers, both the spoken and the unspoken ones.

What is your response to the father? The woman? The crowds? Journal your insights and reflections.

DAY 4

SHOUTING FOR MERCY
Matthew 9:27–34

Place yourself on the road again as two blind men begin to follow Jesus, shouting for mercy and believing that Jesus can heal them. As they leave the house where Jesus is staying, a man who cannot speak is brought in. Jesus restores sight to the blind and speech to the dumb.

The crowd is amazed. The Pharisees condemn Jesus and begin to accuse him of being demon possessed.

What is your response to people who shout out their need in some way? Sit and talk with Jesus about your responses. Journal your insights.

DAY 5

INVITED TO RESPOND
Matthew 9:35–38

Today you begin travelling with Jesus as he ministers in other towns and villages. As you stand and watch, listen closely. How does Jesus see the crowds (v 36)? How does he ask you and his disciples to respond (vv 37–38)?

Journal your response to Jesus' request.

RESPONDING THROUGH REFLECTION

As you come into this time of reflection, ask the Holy Spirit to help you see your week as God sees it. Look over the events of the past seven days. In what areas do you sense God has been present? Ask him to show you where he has indeed been – with you or encountering you through others.

Take some time to reflect on your inner attitudes and feelings. Pay attention to your experiences of love, joy, harmony, freedom. Take note of any experiences of pain, confusion, anger, anxiety, or entrapment.

How is God speaking to you, drawing you, in these experiences? In what ways are you responding to or co-operating with God? In what ways are you not?

What is your prayer now? Is it confession, praise, thanksgiving, petition, intercession?

PREPARING TO SHARE

In your time together with your spiritual friend, take a few minutes to come into each other's presence and the presence of God.

Then share with each other how God has been present to you this week and how you are responding. Is there something you sense you need to focus on? Something to pray about? Or something to act on?

As you grow in trust and openness towards each other, you will be able to ask for each other's prayer support concerning specific areas of inner change, resistance, and growth.

WEEK 7

OUR OUTWARD JOURNEY

PRAYER FOCUS

Lord, help me to trust you for all I need on the outward journey.

COMING

Jesus invites us to come, to be with him, and then to go out. In this time of coming to him, choose a prayer exercise that will help you to be still in body, mind and spirit.

BEING WITH

Last week's readings concluded with Jesus asking his disciples to pray that God would send out people to work in the field of his harvest.

Our concerns become our prayers. In prayer, we hear God. As we listen, we find a way to respond to the concerns God planted within us. This is all the movement of God's Spirit within us. Praying and listening brings us into the place where God is moving.

GO WITHOUT LUGGAGE
Matthew 10:1–15

Jesus is teaching us deep lessons of trust and dependency. He tells his disciples to carry only what he has given them (vv 7–10), to accept the hospitality of others (vv 11–15), and to give what they have been given (vv 8, 12, 19).

What kind of responses do you hear and feel within yourself as you reflect on what Jesus is saying?

GO IN GOD'S CARE
Matthew 10:24–31

In the same way that persons respond to Jesus, so they respond to those who serve him (vv 24–25, and see 9:34; 12:24).

Instead of living within the constricted reality of those who reject and criticise, Jesus invites us to move within the larger reality of God's ability (v 28), God's care (v 29), and God's knowing (v 30).

As members of God's family (v 25), every detail of our need is known to God. Nothing escapes his attention. Just at the time when we feel the most fearful, misunderstood, or rejected, we can remember that we live and move within the great reality. Jesus, once rejected and crucified, is with us now in solidarity.

Take some time in the quiet to speak to God about your fears, your needs. Journal your insights and discoveries.

CARRY A CROSS
Matthew 10:34–39

In God's Kingdom, losing is gaining. That is made clear in these verses where Jesus tells us that he brings a sword (vv 34–36), and those in which he tells us that we must carry a cross (vv 37–39).

As we listen to the lessons for the outward journey, he asks us where our first love and loyalty lie. What does it mean to you to say 'Lord Jesus'? Journal your insights.

DAY 4

JESUS' SOLIDARITY WITH US
Matthew 10:40–42

Jesus identifies closely with those who follow and serve him (vv 40–42). Spend time today waiting in his presence. You may find it helpful to visualise him sitting among his disciples, teaching. Place yourself among the group. Wait and listen.

Record your reflections in your journal.

DAY 5

RETURN AND REST
Matthew 11:25–30

The disciples go out in obedience to Jesus' directions. After completing a time of ministry, they return. (See also Luke 9:1–6, 10.) They are both joyful and tired, and their faith and obedience bring joy to Jesus (vv 25–27).

This is the rhythm of life with Jesus; coming, being with, and being sent out. After being sent out to serve him the disciples return to be with him.

Spend time meditating on verses 28–30. What phrase or word stands out and holds your attention? Stay with that word or phrase, and reflect on it in the quiet.

Allow it to sink into all the corners of your life. Write your responses to God's teaching in your journal.

94

RESPONDING THROUGH REFLECTION

As you reflect over this week, ask the Holy Spirit to help you see your week as God does. Ask the Lord to show you where he has been present in your life – with you or in others.

Take some time to reflect on your inner attitudes and feelings. Pay attention to your experiences of love, joy, harmony, freedom. Take note of any experiences of pain, confusion, anger, anxiety, or entrapment.

How is God speaking to you, drawing you, in these experiences? In what ways are you responding to or co-operating with him? In what ways are you not?

What is your prayer now? Is it confession, praise, thanksgiving, petition, intercession?

PREPARING TO SHARE

In your time with your spiritual friend, take some time to quiet yourselves and to be present to God and to each other. Then share with each other how God has been present to you this week and how you are responding. What do you want to focus on, pray more about, or take action on?

How do you need each other's prayer support? For areas of inner change? Resistance? Or in growth as you keep moving on the outward journey?

WEEK 8

JESUS' EASY YOKE

PRAYER FOCUS

Lord, I take your gentle yoke upon me and learn from you.

COMING

Take some time to place your body, mind, and spirit into the presence of God.

BEING WITH

Here and there in our journey through Matthew's Gospel we have seen the Pharisees and the teachers of the Law criticising Jesus and his followers. In this twelfth chapter, the tension begins to mount. The merciful righteousness and faithfulness to which Jesus calls us (5:20) come into conflict with the legalism of the Pharisees.

On Day 5 last week, our meditation was centred in Jesus' invitation to come and take his yoke upon us. This week we will be seeing the kind of yoke the religious rulers laid on people.

At the end of each 'Being With' period, stay in the presence of Jesus and meditate on his yoke, and what it means to you. Talk with Jesus about it. Listen to him. Record your discoveries in your journal.

FREEDOM VERSUS GUILT
Matthew 12:1–8

As you read the story, reflect on where this event happens and who is there. Listen to the conversation.

What do you learn about the yoke of the Pharisees (vv 2,7)? What do you learn about the easy yoke of Jesus?

Use these words of Jesus as a prayer of meditation.

> Come to me, all of you who are tired from carrying heavy loads, and I will give you rest. Take my yoke and put it on you, and learn from me, because I am gentle and humble in spirit; and you will find rest. For the yoke I will give you is easy, and the load I will put on you is light.
>
> (Matthew 11:28–30 GNB)

Describe your thoughts and the fruit of your meditations in your journal.

HELPING VERSUS LEGALISM
Matthew 12:9–14

It is still the Sabbath. We walk away from the wheat fields and over to the synagogue, still with Jesus and his disciples. As you sit in the synagogue, you notice a man with a paralysed hand. Enter further into the story – listen, see, feel, touch.

Again you are confronted with the contrast between the yoke of the Pharisees, with their legalistic view of what makes a person righteous before God, and the kind yoke of Jesus. Reflect on the differences between the two.

Meditate in prayer using the passage above from Day 1. Write about your experiences and discoveries in your journal.

DAY 3

GENTLENESS IN RESPONSE TO REJECTION
Matthew 12:15–21

A number of times in our journey through Matthew, we have withdrawn with Jesus to escape from places where there were threats on his life (2:13–14, 22–23; 4:12). Now he withdraws again to yield control to God, and the religious leaders take control of the situation by plotting to kill God's Son. But Jesus walks under the yoke of his heavenly Father. It is out of this relationship that he responds.

As you meditate on this passage, what more do you discover about the easy yoke of Jesus? About the gentleness of justice and hope?

In your prayer focus on the yoke passage again and journal your insights from the meditation.

DAY 4

FOR JESUS OR AGAINST?
Matthew 12:22–32

If the Pharisees see themselves as servants of God, then from their perspective, Jesus must be a servant of Satan. So they accuse Jesus of being Satan's tool.

The yokes that we accept and allow to control our understanding of reality can be deadly or life-saving. In verses 31–32, Jesus points out the danger of being weighed down under a yoke that refuses to allow the Holy Spirit to breathe truth and freedom into our thinking. The work of the Spirit is vital to our knowing God and to our being brought into the Kingdom. If we reject the Spirit of God (the Spirit described in verse 18, the Spirit that rests upon Jesus), we reject God's way of bringing us to himself; we reject forgiveness of our sin.

After reading the passage prayerfully several times, spend some time in prayer using the yoke passage from Day 1. Then journal your insights and impressions.

DAY 5

GOOD TREASURE VERSUS BAD
Matthew 12:33–37

Jesus draws us again and again to look within – at our heart. What fills our heart will spill over into what we say and do.

The righteousness of the Pharisees denies there is evil within. The greater faithfulness and righteousness is honest about our heart problem. Under the yoke of Jesus, we are freed to be honest about ourselves, and we are met with kindness and grace. This is the good news: Jesus came to call sinners to himself (9:12–13).

'Happy are those who know they are spiritually poor; the Kingdom of heaven belongs to them!' he told the crowds on the mountain (5:3 GNB).

The judgment referred to in this passage (vv 36–37) applies to words – the outward sign of what is in the heart. As we listen to what we say, we discover what is within.

Jesus calls us to begin discerning where our words and actions come from. Always remember: he meets us with grace and mercy. Living under his yoke will begin to sensitise us to what is within.

In your prayer time, use the yoke passage from Day 1. Journal what you have learned.

DAY 6

RESPONDING THROUGH REFLECTION

As you come into the quiet today, be gentle with yourself in the presence of Jesus. His yoke is easy, kind and light. And he will give you rest.

Ask the Lord to show you where he has been present in your life – with you or in others.

Take some time to reflect on your inner attitudes and feelings. Pay attention to your experiences of love, joy, harmony, or freedom. Note any experiences of pain, confusion, anger, anxiety, or entrapment.

How is God speaking to you, drawing you, in these experiences?

In what ways are you responding to or co-operating with God? In what ways are you not?

What is your prayer now – confession, praise, thanksgiving, petition, intercession?

PREPARING TO SHARE

Listen gently and carefully to each other as you share this week's discoveries about Jesus' yoke and your inner heart. Listen prayerfully to what God is saying to you and how you are responding to him.

Where do you sense you need to focus attention, to pray or to take action?

WEEK 9

LEARNING TO TRUST

PRAYER FOCUS

Lord, help me to recognise you in time of crisis.

COMING

You are continuing in the rhythm of coming, being with and going out. This is the time of coming – of walking away from activity to be with God. Settle yourself in God's presence. Use a prayer exercise if you find one helpful.

BEING WITH

Meditation . . . is alternately 'a dance' and 'a fight', or else it is both at once. But we continually turn to it for renewal and to find tranquility after the rush and worry of action. I refer not only to the worry that arises from our sinful lusts, but also that which is inseparable from even the sincerest vocation of service . . . Meditation makes us independent of events, by making us dependent upon God.[1]

HEARING AND UNDERSTANDING
Matthew 13:1–9, 18–23

The parable of the sower and the seed is about four different soils. As we dig a bit deeper into what Jesus was saying, we realise that the soils are four different ways of hearing God.

- The seed on the path represents those who hear and don't understand. The Evil One snatches away what they hear (vv 4, 19).
- The rocky ground represents those who hear, but the word does not sink deeply into them (vv 5, 20). When trouble comes, they give up quickly.
- The thorn bushes speak of a person who hears, but the worry about this life and a love for riches chokes off any growth (vv 7, 22).
- The seed in good soil is for those who hear and understand – and bear fruit (vv 8, 23).

Trust in God is closely tied to how we hear and understand. Take some time in your meditation on this text to listen to what God is sowing in your heart. Such meditation allows the Word of God to sink into the soil of our heart and bear fruit.

Record your insights and discoveries in your journal.

DAY 2

RELINQUISHING CONTROL
Matthew 14:1–21

The outward journey of obedience will lead us to places where our trust in God and God's greater purpose and reality will help us find meaning in the face of loss and in the face of human weakness.

After he hears of John's death, Jesus withdraws. But even as he seeks the quiet of solitude, the crowd is waiting for him. In response to his followers' need for food at the end of the day, the disciples want nothing more than to avoid getting involved. But Jesus draws them back into the situation and presses them for a response.

When similar situations happen in our lives, they strip us of our ability to cope on our own. Our resources are small, human, and limited (v 17). The disciples learned that they did not have to have control. They did not need to cope alone. By offering up what they have to Jesus they release their gifts and themselves to his control. The outcome is in his hands. He takes, he blesses, he breaks, and he gives, Jesus is helping them learn to trust.

In your contemplation of this story, walk into the event. Sit with the disciples and listen to the response to Jesus' compassion on the multitude (vv 14–15).

What does he ask from you? What do you have to give? Note in your journal what you are learning about trust and about control.

DAY 3

BOUTS OF 'LITTLE FAITH'
Matthew 14:22–33

Once again, obeying Jesus has brought his disciples to a fearful, stormy place. Jesus has been encountering his own inner and outer storms (14:1–3, 10–13, 22–23). Now he comes to the disciples who had done his bidding and found the wind and waves against them (v 24). They are terrified.

The life of discipleship is susceptible to bouts of little faith . . . Nevertheless, Jesus does not abandon his disciples at such times but stands ever ready with

103

his saving power to sustain them so that they can in fact discharge the mission he has entrusted to them.[2]

As you contemplate this story, place yourself in the event. What are the boat and the storm for you? Who is Jesus for you in this (vv 28, 30, 33)? Where do you find yourself experiencing bouts of 'little faith'? Journal your insights.

DAY 4

WALKING IN FREEDOM
Matthew 15:1–9

If we are honest with ourselves, most of us have a deep need to please others. When pleasing others comes into conflict with following and obeying Christ, we can feel caught in a dilemma. Jesus helps us discern between human rules and his Word (v 9). As you meditate on this story, what is God saying to you? Journal your response.

DAY 5

EXPOSING WHAT IS WITHIN
Matthew 15:10–20

Only Jesus can set us free from our inner self (Romans 5:1–5). He came to be with us and he came to rescue us from the slavery of sin (1:21, 23).

As you meditate on these verses, stay with the word or phrase that holds your attention. Allow it to sink into your thinking, understanding, and your inner self. Journal your discoveries.

DAY 6

RESPONDING THROUGH REFLECTION

As you look back over your week and your journal entries, do you find any patterns emerging? What are you learning about yourself? About trust? About Jesus?

Ask God to show you where he has been present in your life – with you or in others.

Take some time to reflect on your experiences of love, joy, harmony, and freedom. Note any experiences of pain, confusion, anger, anxiety, or entrapment.

How is God speaking to you, drawing you, in these experiences? What kind of prayer do you want to pray – confession, praise, thanksgiving, petition, intercession?

PREPARING TO SHARE

Begin listening for patterns in each other's lives. Maybe you will not see one. We cannot make happen what is not there. Listen for each other's trust in God and the trusting responses you are making.

THINKING GOD-THOUGHTS

PRAYER FOCUS

Lord, help me to think your thoughts.

COMING

Take some time to bring your body, mind, and spirit into the quiet presence of God. Allow any busy thoughts to slip away; rest any heavy thoughts in God's presence.

BEING WITH

One of the tasks of discipleship is to distinguish truth from untruth. Jesus speaks of this as thinking the things of God as opposed to thinking the things of humankind (16:23). We find Jesus continually discerning both the distance and the difference between the two and teaching his disciples to discern as he does.

DAY 1

FEEDING OUR THOUGHTS
Matthew 13:33, 16:5–12

A woman began a dialogue with God. One of the first needs she admitted was her desire to know him more

107

closely. She further admitted that she felt far from him. Then she listened. The response she heard was this: 'Maybe you should give up reading the newspaper for an hour after breakfast. Maybe you should spend that time with me.'

At first she was surprised that God had spoken. And then she pondered what he had said. She decided to heed his advice and to read the newspaper at another time in the day. After breakfast she would spend time with him and listen to him. Her relationship with him grew, and she began to read the newspaper with new insight.

In the quiet, get in touch with your own desire for God. Talk to him about it.

DAY 2

RETREATING TO THE MOUNTAINS
Matthew 16:13–20

Climb the mountain with Jesus and his other disciples today. As you sit on the grassy slopes, listen to Jesus' questions. What is your answer? Who is Jesus for you?

We know the answer Peter gave, but what is the answer that grows out of our own experience of walking with him and having him walk with us?

Write about your walk with Jesus in your journal.

DAY 3

FOLLOWING MEANS SUFFERING
Matthew 16:21–28

Stay on the mountain today and reflect deeply as you hear Jesus telling you the cost of following him. What kind of thoughts do you hear within yourself? What is the cross for you (v 24)?

Be honest before God in your journal, and bring your

responses to him. Then seek to discern whether they are from God or from your human nature.

DAY 4

LISTENING
Matthew 17:1–13, 22–23

We are allowed to join Peter, James and John as Jesus leads them up another high mountain. There, away from the crowds, in the quiet of the mountain, God meets with them.

Guided retreats and quiet days ... encourage both intimate relaxation and struggle with the Real One welling up in and around us. They can offer protected respites from the breathless driveness of culture and ego.[1]

We can get caught up in the spiritual experience for itself and overlook God, who is present. God stills the clutching excitement of the disciples as he draws their attention back to listening to Jesus. Be present to Jesus now. Simply be attentive and listen.

Record what you hear in your journal.

DAY 5

THINKING THE THOUGHTS OF GOD
Romans 12:1–2

As you meditate on these words, reflect also on what Jesus says about the shape of discipleship (Matthew 16:24–27) – its cost and its rewards. We carry a cross and live in hope – walking like Jesus in the greater reality of the Resurrection (v 21) and Jesus' Second Coming.

Record some of your reflections in your journal.

DAY 6

RESPONDING THROUGH REFLECTION

Reflect today on what you have been hearing this week.

Ask the Lord to show you where he has been present in your life – with you or in others.

Take some time to reflect on your inner attitudes and feelings. Pay attention to your experiences of love, joy, harmony, or freedom. Note any experiences of pain, confusion, anger, anxiety, or entrapment.

How is God speaking to you, drawing you, in these experiences? What is your prayer today?

PREPARING TO SHARE

In your time with your spiritual friend, share from your prayer experiences this week. How are you learning to think God-thoughts? What blocks are you discovering that hinder your responses to God?

LETTING GO

PRAYER FOCUS

Lord, help me to see as you see.

COMING

Take a few minutes to bring yourself into God's presence.

BEING WITH

'Whoever wishes to become great among you must be your servant, and whoever wishes to be first among you must be slave of all. For the Son of Man came not to be served but to serve, and to give his life a ransom for many.' (Mark 10:43–45)

DAY 1

LETTING GO OF CONTROL
Matthew 18:6–14

Jesus shifts his focus from the child (vv 1–5) to the children who believe in him – his followers. Our return to God and our belonging in God's household is the reason Jesus came among us.

Hence the startling anger and seriousness with which Jesus warns the one who places a stumbling block in the path of our journey to and with God, whether another person or our own lifestyle choices (vv 6–9). We are to search for the one who does stumble and fall until that one is found and restored (vv 10–14).

As you meditate prayerfully on this passage, what word or phrase catches your attention? Stay with it and allow it to sink gently into the rooms and relationships of your life. Write your response to God in your journal.

DAY 2

LETTING GO OF REVENGE
Matthew 18:15–35

We go to our brother or sister who wrongs us, not to condemn or get even, but to restore the relationship – to make peace (5:9). We cannot control the response of the other person (vv 16–17), but we are instructed to guard our own attitude (vv 21–22, 35).

It may be that you feel some hesitation or distance between yourself and your spiritual friend or between you and another person in the community of faith. As you wait in God's presence, bring that person and yourself to God. What resistance do you discover within yourself? What desire for peace is there, if any? Make a note of your reflection in your journal.

DAY 3

LETTING GO OF EGO
Matthew 19:1–15

After being in retreat in the mountains, Jesus and his disciples journey south. In the presence of God, Jesus receives strength and direction. Now they begin the long walk to Jerusalem.

On the road he is met by Pharisees who come to test him with a question: May a man divorce his wife for any cause? (At that time a man could divorce his wife, among other things, for burning his evening meal.) Jesus looks beyond the narrow and hard attitude and behind the question, and the contemporary view of women. He points, instead, to God's creation of both men and women and in so doing reminds his hearers of the image of God within each person, whether male or female.

As children are brought to him to be blessed, the disciples forget the lesson he has just taught them (18:1–5). He rebukes their hasty response and with simple hospitality makes space for the young. Jesus embraces and blesses the powerless.

Place yourself in the story, join the disciples on the road to Jerusalem. Who do you find yourself standing close to? What do you need from Jesus? Who are the powerless you can bless in your life? Record your insights and discoveries in your journal.

DAY 4

REMOVING STUMBLING BLOCKS
Matthew 19:16–30

A young man comes up to Jesus and asks how to receive eternal life. Jesus finally puts his finger on the one thing that is a stumbling block in the path of this man's journey to God: his wealth (v 21).

As you wait in the presence of Jesus, ask him 'How do you view my life? What stumbling blocks do you see?' Record in your journal what you hear God saying to you.

114

LETTING GO OF LIFE
Matthew 20:17–28

The disciples are unable to grasp that greatness in the Kingdom of Heaven means serving others in the same way Jesus served. Service for Jesus included giving his life. What does it entail for you? Make a note of your discoveries in your journal.

RESPONDING THROUGH REFLECTION

The closer we come to the cross, the more we are confronted with the parts of our lives that need to be laid down out of love for Jesus. Place yourself on the road to Jerusalem with Jesus today. Walk with him, listen to him. Reflect on what you have learned.

Ask the Lord to show you where God has been present in your life – with you or in others. Take some time to reflect on your inner attitudes and feelings. Note your experiences of love, joy, harmony, and freedom. Pay attention to any experiences of pain, confusion, anger, anxiety, or entrapment. How is God speaking to you, drawing you, in these experiences? What is your prayer today?

PREPARING TO SHARE

From time to time you may be feeling some distance, some hesitation between you and your spiritual friend. Bring this gently into the space between you today, along with your prayer experience. Listen carefully to each other as you share what God is saying to you and reflect on how you are each responding to him.

JOURNEY TO THE CROSS

PRAYER FOCUS

Lord, help me to stay with you.

COMING

Relax, be still and attentive in God's presence.

BEING WITH

'You will name him Jesus – because he will save his people from their sins' (Matthew 1:21, GNB).

DAY 1

'YOUR KING IS COMING'
Matthew 21:1–17

As you enter Jerusalem with Jesus, notice who is present and how they respond to the Saviour. Where do you find yourself standing? Who do you find yourself identifying with? Note in your journal something of your own prayer experience.

DAY 2

'I WANTED, BUT YOU WOULD NOT'
Matthew 23:37–39; 26:1–16

Throughout the story at this point, Matthew traces two distinct movements for us: one is the mounting rejection fueling the plot against Jesus' life; the other is the steady love Jesus has for God and for people as he walks towards the cross.

Enter the story slowly, prayerfully. Stay in the place where you find yourself meeting Jesus. Write about your prayer experience in your journal.

DAY 3

'THIS IS MY BLOOD . . . POURED OUT FOR THE FORGIVENESS OF SINS'
Matthew 26:17–35

Like so many mealtimes before, Jesus takes the bread, gives thanks, breaks it and gives it to his friends. Watch him do this and bear in mind that this is the last time he will do this before the cross and the breaking of his body. Now watch him take the wine, listen as he gives thanks for it and, like the disciples, receive it from his own hands. Listen as he tells you that this is his blood shed for you – that it seals the new covenant. Reflect on the fact that the old covenant is fulfilled and the new one is beginning.

Be aware of your feelings as you are present at the Last Supper and record these in your journal. Then remind yourself that Jesus knows our weaknesses and our capacity to betray him (v 31) yet he invites us to meet him in Galilee (v 32). How do you react to the fact that we are always welcomed back because Jesus' giving of himself has made a way for us to come? Write a prayer of response in your journal.

DAY 4

'NOT WHAT I WANT BUT WHAT YOU WANT'
Matthew 26:36–56

Obedience costs. But when we say, 'Not what I want but what you want', we are not alone. Jesus has knelt on the ground too. But, as he did, we may well walk in that obedience alone (vv 31, 57).

Walk quietly in the story today. Wait in the garden in the presence of God. What is your prayer? Who is Jesus for you? You may want to write your prayer in your journal.

DAY 5

'TRULY THIS MAN WAS GOD'S SON'
Matthew 27:27–61

Stripped, made fun of, spat upon, led out, crucified. Accused, insulted, mocked by the people, abandoned by God. Jesus gave a loud cry and breathed his last.

When he gave himself on the cross, in seeming weakness, the centurion became convinced that Jesus was who he was: God's Son.

Sit before the cross. Watch and wait. Record your feelings in your journal.

DAY 6

RESPONDING THROUGH REFLECTION

As you come into the quiet today, ask the Holy Spirit to help you see your week as God does. Where have you been in your prayer? What have you seen? For what are you thankful? Where have you seen God – in others, in the larger world, in yourself?

How is God drawing you through your experiences of love, joy, and harmony? In your experiences of pain, confusion, anger, or anxiety?

In what ways are you responding to God? Write about these in your journal.

PREPARING TO SHARE

Reflect carefully on what you would like to share about your prayer and life experience this week. Be listening for what God is saying and for how you are responding.

Soon the three-month journey will be complete. Pray and talk together about where you go from here. Do you want to continue to journey alongside each other in the months that lie ahead? Or do you feel your spiritual friendship has run its course for now?

WEEK 13

JESUS: WITH US UNTIL THE END OF THE AGE

PRAYER FOCUS

Lord, help me to live in faith, hope, and love.

COMING

Gently relax and allow any tension to fall away as you open yourself to God's presence with you.

BEING WITH

'He will be called Emmanuel (which means "God is with us") (Matthew 1:23, GNB)

'Go, then, to all peoples. And I will be with you always to the end of the age.' (Matthew 28:19–20, GNB).

DAY 1

JESUS: WITH YOU ALWAYS
Matthew 28:1–20

The eleven are commissioned by Jesus to go on the great outward journey. Beginning in Jerusalem and moving out into the world, they walk under the authority of Jesus Christ and the greater reality of God's Kingdom to make disciples of all nations. From those early days after the Resurrection right down through the centuries, each faithful disciple told first one and then another, and so the message has come to us today.

Think of those people who link your faith journey to the journey of those early women and men. Take a moment to thank God for their faithfulness.

Spend some time reflecting on your own outward journey. What is the Risen Jesus nudging you to do? Where does this outward journey take you?

Remember that even in the journey of your searching for direction, Jesus is 'with you always, to the end of the age'.

DAY 2

LIVING IN HOPE
Matthew 24:3–14

The disciples asked Jesus about the present age. How long would it last? What would be the sign of Jesus' return and of the end of this age?

We live in a world of chaotic political upheavals, with 'nation (rising) against nation, and kingdom against kingdom' and there are 'famines and earthquakes in various places' (v 7). Jesus foresaw these events and told his followers about them but drew their attention away from being alarmed in the midst of the chaos – for the chaos is not the end. Jesus is Lord of the end, and 'the end is not yet' (v8). He goes on to describe what will happen to those who are faithful, and what the state of the world will become 'because of the increase of lawlessness' (v 12). But again, he draws our attention away from the violence and anarchy to simple faithfulness to Jesus Christ and the proclamation of the good news in all the world. Then the end will come (v 14).

Jesus is not instructing his followers to ignore war, violence and chaos; to somehow remove themselves from the pain and terrible anxiety people live in from day to day. Rather, he is calling us not to be controlled by what seems chaotic and uncontrollable but to stay with him in simple trust.

Julian of Norwich lived in England during a century of tumult and crisis: great schisms in the church, the Hundred Years' War between England and France, the chaos of the Peasants Revolt, and even the overrunning of Norwich itself by rebels. Through all of this, she stayed close to God, and could say:

> Just so (our Lord) said in the last words, with perfect fidelity, alluding to us all: You will not be overcome ... And these words: You will not be overcome, were said very insistently and strongly, for certainty and strength against every tribulation which may come. He did not say: You will not be troubled, you will not be belaboured, you will not be disquieted; but he said: You will not be overcome.[1]

Reflect quietly on Julian's listenings and on where you find your hope in the face of world chaos. Record your reflection in your journal.

WATCHING FOR HIS COMING
Matthew 24:29–31, 36–44

The disciples asked Jesus when he would return. Down through the years many people have sought to set a date. But Jesus draws our attention away from date-setting (v 36) and helps us understand that such knowledge is not available to us. Rather he calls us to be faithful and to 'stay awake' (v 42).

The faithful practice of spiritual disciplines helps us to be aware of God, to be awake to where he is present, and to recognise how we are responding. Gradually our hearts are emptied of the world's clutter that we think we have to have for our happiness and security. The emphasis creates an open space for hope, love and faithfulness to grow and be at home. We will notice an intensifying in our longing for his return and to see him as he is (1 John 3:2–3).

As you meditate on these teachings of Jesus, what words or phrases stand out for you? Stay with these words, let them settle into your heart and life.

DAY 4

FAITHFUL UNTIL HE COMES
Matthew 25:1–30

Notice that the master gives the talents, entrusting what was his to the servants. Jesus describes two responses. Two servants were faithful; one was afraid and simply buried his talent in the earth.

The parable is designed for us to reflect:

- on large gifts and small
- the Giver

- our use of gifts while we wait for the Master's return
- being trustworthy with what we have
- the Master's joy

All we have and are is a gift from God. We are simply stewards. God is the owner.

Spend some time in quiet in God's presence after asking the question: Lord, in what way do I live and serve to bring you joy? Write down what God says.

DAY 5

CARING FOR CHRIST'S FAMILY
Matthew 25:31–46

In various places in Matthew, Jesus has emphasised his solidarity with those who follow him. 'Whoever does the will of my Father in heaven is my brother and sister and mother' (12:50). He calls his disciples members 'of his household' (10:25). Jesus so identifies with his followers as they live and serve in this present age that the person who welcomes them, gives them something to eat or drink, clothes them or takes care of them while they are sick, or visits them in prison is welcomed: 'Come, you that are blessed by my Father!' (25:34). Some will be truly surprised. While serving a simple meal or making space in their lives and home for the unexpected visitor who is Christ's brother or sister, they have made space for Jesus.

So we are to be on the lookout for strangers, for the most humble of his sisters and brothers, and for angels – those messengers who are followers of Jesus. Such hospitality allows Jesus in and is a blessing to us, to the one we welcome, and to God. One way of being faithful until Jesus comes is to make space for people to be fed, clothed, cared for, and visited when ill or in prison, as one missionary couple found.

When the phone rang in their Frankfurt apartment, the young wife was not happy to hear that she and her husband were to receive company from Czechoslovakia that weekend. She and her husband wondered how they could make space in an already overcrowded three-room apartment, but, reluctantly she agreed.

When the visitor, Ernst Schmucker, arrived, his radiant smiling face, his gentle presence, and his deep inner joy breathed light and hope into the lives of the two tired mission workers. Ernst had endured the communist takeover of his country, frequent interrogations, and constant surveillance. He lived in the hope and the joy of Jesus' coming. As he told his story, the children and their parents listened and rejoiced with him.

One afternoon, while Ernst was visiting the city, the four-year-old son woke up from his nap and wandered into the kitchen. 'Where's Jesus?' he asked.

'Jesus?' responded his mother.

'Yes, Jesus. Where's the Jesus man?' he asked again.

The young mother smiled and felt a deep sense of joy and strength springing up within her. How glad she was that they had said 'Yes, Mr Schmucker can come'.

As you reflect on Jesus' teaching, who are the 'angels' who have appeared at your door in your life? How did you respond?

DAY 6

RESPONSE THROUGH REFLECTION

Spiritual friendship is a profound act of hospitality. As we graciously receive each other, we are also looking for God in our journeys. And as we begin to see God in each other, we become aware of God in those around us and in the larger world.

What kind of encouragement do you need to be faithful?

How has meeting with a spiritual friend helped you? How has God revealed himself in your times of quiet and in the rest of your life this week?

PREPARING TO SHARE

After a period of quiet prayer, take time to listen to each other's journey and experience of the last three months. Be present and receptive to each other as you explore what you need as you continue on your journey.

What helps you to be aware of Jesus' presence with you (28:20)? In what ways are you ready to continue meeting with a spiritual friend? In what ways are you not? What commitments are you open to exploring?

PART FIVE

ONGOING SPIRITUAL FRIENDSHIP

CHAPTER 8

THE NEXT STEP

> No relationship is static, and all our relation-
> ships, insofar as they are under the guidance of
> the Holy Spirit, move more and more towards
> spiritual friendship. They move in that direction
> simply because this is the kind of God Chris-
> tians believe in . . . God is friendship. We are
> made after [God's] image.[1]

If you have travelled this far with a spiritual friend
or a small group you may be wondering where to
go from here. The guide based on Matthew's Gospel
is only one of many different ways of setting some
kind of structure for your time together. You may
have ideas of your own about what you would like
to focus on next.

During the times of reading, reflection, and sharing, some discover an area of their lives that needs
attention. Sometimes there is just a sense of the
need to continue. Either way, God is nudging us
on. This call is our highest adventure. It is on this
journey that we will know our greatest battles and
our fullest joys.

While the Scriptures do not place the battle at
the centre – only Jesus can ever hold that place in
God's great reality – even a casual reading of the
biblical account makes it clear to us that knowing
God and living in harmony with him is no easy task.

We are confronted with enemies from without and from within.[2] However, God has not planned for us to journey alone, even though in the deepest sense, our journey is only our own. We cannot journey for another. But the companionship of another who is also walking in the Way is both comforting and strengthening. The presence of others who are in the believing community is for our good.[3]

If you are unsure as to your next step, listen prayerfully to your inner heart and spirit and open yourself to God's gentle guidance. Are there entries in your journal that you would like to explore more fully with a spiritual friend? What needs are you aware of? What longings do you hear?

You may decide to continue for a time – maybe to covenant to walk together for a year – with the person with whom you explored Matthew's Gospel. You may decide you would like to share your journey with another.

* * *

One woman discovered a readiness to look more closely at her personal pilgrimage. She sensed God was inviting her to walk further on her inward journey. Such exploration is often accompanied by an openness to be more present to another, and she invited a friend to consider a mutual journey into their respective childhoods, paying attention to pain, dysfunction, comfort, and strengths.

These women trusted God's gentle, healing presence to accompany them as they chose a book to read and met weekly to hear each other's discoveries.

One man became aware of his need for more time in prayer and solitude as he began practising spiritual disciplines during the course. He wondered how to balance his schedule of work, family and church involvement to include the space he desired for being present to God. But he also wondered about his identity: where did he look for affirmation and acceptance – to other men and their production-filled life or to God? What if someone asked him about his schedule, and he admitted he needed more time for prayer? Would he be understood? What did this tug on his inner person mean? He decided to explore these questions and others with a spiritual friend.

Another woman felt God inviting her to respond to the movement of God's presence in her life by writing to a friend and asking her to enter into spiritual friendship with her. At first her friend was hesitant, but as the first woman continued to write and to explain what she was learning and appreciating about such a relationship, the friend agreed. These women correspond regularly. In their letters they include whatever they feel comfortable sharing from their journals, prayer requests, and responses to some of the questions included in 'Guidelines for a Spiritual Friendship'.[4] (See page 138.) They try to meet together every three months.

Two other women meet about every three weeks. One is beginning to share what she is discovering as she learns to pray out of her experiences. For years she had begun her prayers where she thought God and the church wanted her to be. Now, as a widow who is adjusting to living alone and to taking more responsibility for practical, everyday, and business decisions, she is finding a new restfulness as she discovers and relates to God's presence in her daily experience and her responses to the everyday. The other woman is seeking God's direction as she listens to nudgings in her life to leave her present vocation and return to school. Both women find a common bond as they share their experiences of transition and change.

A husband and wife set aside an hour and a half a week to wait in God's presence in silent prayer, then to record in their journal what they sense they have heard. During the last half-hour, they listen attentively as they read their journal entries to each other.

Two men meet about once a month to discuss what they are receiving through the reading of other spiritual writers and how their relationships at work, in their families, and with God are being touched.

One woman finds that as she makes regular hospital visits to a family member during an extended life-threatening illness, she is learning to listen as a spiritual friend and is more able to be present to the pain, uncertainty, and waiting along with others in the hospital who also wait.

Two male students committed themselves to meet for lunch once a week. Their main focus was to assist each other to remember to be present to God in the tight schedule between work, classes, readings, assignments, and family responsibilities.

Two mothers of teenage children meet together at a quiet table in a coffee shop once a week to be accountable to each other. Their conversation as spiritual friends includes how they are living out their love of God for themselves, and for their nearly-adult offspring. They, too, use the 'Guidelines for Spiritual Friendship' as a starting point and move out from there.

A group of women who live and serve in mission work in several different countries around the world acknowledged their need for support and for spiritual friendship. In addition to the group letters they write every month, each embarked on a spiritual friendship with another. Two of these women agreed to pray for each other daily, to write once a month, and to meet for a week-end of retreat once a quarter. The days for retreat include time for meditation on Scripture, silent prayer, journaling and sharing their journals and journeys together.[5]

Two men meet once a week for seventy-five minutes to read and meditate on the coming Sunday's lectionary reading, using *lectio divina* as a way of allowing the Scripture to move from their head into their hearts and lives.

* * *

A number of books and cassettes have been produced to promote our spiritual formation. If you find that your needs are slightly different from those of your spiritual friend, you may decide to read separate books but agree to meet to listen to each other's journey. But remember that, in all of our journeying, our primary spiritual guide is the Holy Spirit. The Spirit of Jesus will continue to create the quiet centre within us – the place of meeting, of being listened to, of listening, and of restful companionship.

* * *

If you love me, you will keep my commandments. And I will ask the Father, and he will give you another Advocate, to be with you forever. This is the Spirit of truth, whom the world cannot receive, because it neither sees him nor knows him. You know him, because he abides with you, and he will be in you (John 14:15–17).

Guidelines for Spiritual Friendship

PREPARATION

1. Arrange for time, place, length of session; agree upon who will be the focus of a session at any given time.

2. Pray for the sessions in advance asking God's direction. Pray regularly for one another.

PARTICIPATION

Shared awareness

Begin the sessions with silence (2 to 3 minutes).

Shared presence

1. Be attentive to your friend. Listen . . .
   Openly – rather than being immediately directive.
   Compassionately – rather than being too corrective.
   Reflectively – rather than being compulsive.
   With observations – rather than too many conclusions.
   With clarifying questions – rather than being closed or curious.

2. Be attentive to God's workings in each other's life by reflecting together upon questions such as:

   How has God been at work in my life this week?
   What have been the signs of God's grace to me?
   What images/awareness of God have been helpful to me?
   What may have blocked God's voice to me this week?
   Where might I have failed to experience God's grace?
   What sin do I need to confess?

3. Be attentive to God's immediate presence in your friend's life by asking reflective questions such as:

How is God being with you now?
What is God saying to you now?
How is God motivating/energizing/transforming you?
How are you responding to God in your life now?

Encourage time for 'waiting' before the Lord.

Shared commitments

Be attentive to your friend's need for accountability by asking:

What decisions do I want and need to make in the week to come?
What action to take, prayers to pray; reflection to do?
What changes are being called for in my life?
For what do I want and need to be held accountable till we meet again?

Shared closure

Prayers of acknowledgement, confession, petition, silence, thanksgiving, and intercession.

Additional areas upon which you may focus

Sharing in the spiritual friendship could include:

My spiritual pilgrimage.
My experience of God.
My images of (names for, and how I see) God.
My patterns of communication with God (prayer experience).
My relationship with others or with the church.
How I experience the world.
Areas for spiritual growth in my life.

NOTES

Chapter 1
1. Acts 9:10–19.
2. Acts 9:26–28.
3. Acts 8:26–35.
4. Psalm 42:1–2.
5. Tilden Edwards, *Spiritual Friend* (New York: Paulist Press, 1981) p 16.
6. Philippians 1:6; 2:13.
7. Romans 12:1–2; Galatians 4:19; 5:16–26; Philippians 2:5ff.
8. Eugene Peterson, *Working The Angles* (Michigan: Eerdmans Publishing Co., 1987) p 104.

Chapter 2
1. Margaret Guenther, 'Attending To The Holy', address given at the Spiritual Directors' International Symposium, Baltimore, MD, May 1992. She expands the idea of attention to God in a recent book, *Holy Listening* (London: Darton, Longman and Todd Ltd., 1992).
2. Edwards, *Spiritual Friend*, p 101.
3. Ibid., pp 101–102.
4. Ibid., p101.

Chapter 3
1. Edwards, *Spiritual Friend*, p 121.
2. Ibid., p 105.
3. Peterson, *Working the Angles*, p 118.
4. Aelred of Rievaulx, 'Marriage and the Contemplative Life', *Spiritual Friendship* (Washington, D.C.: Consortium Press, 1974).

Chapter 4
1. Edwards, *Spiritual Friend*, p 129.
2. Marcus Smucker, Marlene Kropf, Erland Waltner, 'Guidelines for Spiritual Friendship', Associated Mennonite Biblical Seminaries, 1989.

Chapter 5
1. William A. Barry, SJ, *Finding God in All Things* (Indiana: Ave Maria Press, 1991) p 21.
2. Luke 5:8–10.

Chapter 6
1. Richard J. Foster, *Celebration of Discipline* (London: Hodder and Stoughton, 1978) p 13.
2. Henri J.M. Nouwen, *Clowning in Rome* (New York: Doubleday Image Books, 1979), p 103.
3. Mark 3:13–14 (Good News Bible).
4. Tilden Edwards, *Living in the Presence* (New York: Harper & Row, 1987), p 22.
5. Several tapes have been produced to help people to come into stillness. See the bibliography on p 143.
6. Anne Broyles, *Journaling: A Spirit Journey* (Nashville, TN: The Upper Room, 1988), and Joseph F. Schmidt, *Praying our Experiences* (Minnesota: Saint Mary's Press, 1989) are both helpful resources.
7. *The Spiritual Exercises of St Ignatius,* trans. Louis J. Puhl (Loyola University Press, 1968). A helpful companion to the *Spiritual Exercises* is *Finding God in All Things* by William A. Barry, SJ.
8. Foster, *Celebration of Discipline*, p 29.
9. Elizabeth O'Connor, *Letters to Scattered Pilgrims* (New York: Harper & Row, 1979), p39.

Week 2
1. Author unknown. Fifteenth-century poem.

Week 4
1. Foster, *Celebration of Discipline*, pp 54–55.

Week 5

1. Jack Dean Kingsbury, *Matthew as Story* (Pennsylvania: Fortress Press, 1986), p 29.

Week 9

1. Paul Tournier, *The Person Reborn* (New York: Harper & Row, 1966), pp 184–85.
2. Kingsbury, *Matthew as Story*, p 134.

Week 10

1. Edwards, *Spiritual Friend*, p 95.

Week 13

1. Julian of Norwich, *Showings*, trans. by Edmund Colledge and James Walsh (London: S.P.C.K., 1978), p 315.

Chapter 8

1. Alan Jones, *Exploring Spiritual Direction* (New York: HarperCollins, 1982), p 4.
2. Ephesians 6:10–18; James 1:12–16; Matthew 15: 10–20.
3. Ephesians 4:11–16.
4. Smucker, Kropf, Waltner, 'Guidelines for Spiritual Friendship'.
5. Linda Shelly, 'A Support Circle', *WMSC Voice,* May 1991, pp 10–11, published by Women's Missionary and Service Commission of the Mennonite Church (Ohio: Bluffton).

Appendix

1. These guidelines are used by students at Associated Mennonite Biblical Seminaries in Elkhart, Indiana, and at Eastern Mennonite Seminary in Harrisonburg, Virginia. They were developed in September of 1989 by Marcus Smucker, Marlene Kropf, and Erland Waltner, faculty members who teach and give spiritual direction at AMBS. The author is grateful for their permission to reprint them.

BIBLIOGRAPHY

For help with listening skills:
Listening by Anne Long (DLT 1990).
Listening to Others by Joyce Huggett (Hodder and Stoughton 1988) chapters 5 and 6.
Holy Listening by Margaret Guenther (DLT 1992).

For futher information of methods of meditation:
Open to God by Joyce Huggett (Hodder and Stoughton 1989).

Further material for meditation:
while on holiday: *Holy Days and Holidays* by Joyce Huggett (BRF 1993).

during Lent: *God's Springtime* by Joyce Huggett (BRF 1992 with accompanying cassette published by Eagle).

Further helpful resource material
To help become more still: *Coming to God* by Jim Borst (Eagle 1992).

Keeping a Spiritual Journal ed. Edward England (Highland Books 1991) where Jenny Cooke, Jennifer Rees Larcombe, Anne Long, Sister Margaret Magdalene and others spell out the value, and suggest methods of keeping a journal.

The Exploring Prayer Series
Edited by Joyce Huggett

Each book in the *Exploring Prayer Series* uses the author's
hard-won experience to point the reader to God – the One
who listens and answers. Authors have been encouraged
to draw upon their own Church tradition so that all can
benefit from the riches of the various strands of the Church:
catholic, evangelical and charismatic. The photographs in
each book have been chosen to reinforce the text.

Angela Ashwin
PATTERNS NOT PADLOCKS

Prayer for parents and all busy people, suggesting practical
ideas and initiatives for prayer building on the chaotic,
busyness of everyday life.

James Borst
COMING TO GOD

A stage by stage introduction to a variety of ways of using
times of stillness, quiet and contemplative meditation.

Michael Mitton
THE SOUNDS OF GOD

Helpful hints on hearing the voice of God, drawn from the
contemplative, evangelical and charismatic traditions.

Gerald O'Mahony
FINDING THE STILL POINT

Writing from his own experience of severe mood
swings, the author provides a means to understand
erratic moods and feelings so as to find the 'still' point, a
safe haven.

Heather Ward
STREAMS IN DRY LAND

Praying when God is distant, when you feel bored or
frustrated with your prayer life – or even empty, arid and
deserted by God.

Joyce Huggett
FINDING GOD IN THE FAST-LANE

A celebration of busyness: ways in which Christians can
today – like Brother Lawrence – gradually learn to enjoy
constant intimacy with God